Two Year

Journey Through
East Africa

East Africa Journey

Willie B. Armstead

authorHOUSE®

AuthorHouse™
1663 Liberty Drive
Bloomington, IN 47403
www.authorhouse.com
Phone: 1-800-839-8640

First published by AuthorHouse   11/16/2011

ISBN: 978-1-4685-0619-8 (sc)
ISBN: 978-1-4685-0618-1 (hc)
ISBN: 978-1-4685-0617-4 (ebk)

Library of Congress Control Number: 2011961126

Printed in the United States of America

Mount Kenya

Safari Club

The Shoreplace of Africa

The Atmosphere of visiting East Africa

Always leave memory of its Primeual Beauty

The African People and there Customs

Tribal Problems Chief Answers

Chief Console

Mrs. Willie B. Armstead

Started writing this book Sunday night

Of January 1st – 8th, 1972

2nd Sun. in Jan.

3rd – 8th 1972

Am writing to let the Negroes of America, know the truth about the nineteen months that I stayed in Mombasa Kenya, East Africa. I didn't find the true hospitality in Africa, that I have always heard mention here in American on Television and elsewhere by the American Negro people. First we are not tribal minded, there is no mark of any kind on our body from my father at birth and not father one of my father children.

No child in America is marked like a pig or calf or dog at birth from his or her father. We have nothing in common; I am talking about African's and American. We don't talk alike, we don't dress alike, we don't cook alike, we don't eat alike, we don't have know chief to go to for information. We are not tribal, we are on different social bases, we don't dance alike, we know nothing about their dance, and they know nothing about ours.

We believe in God they believe in chief, but I am not expecting to get through to some people but I do have proof of everything that I am writing. My main reason for writing this book is that there are so many people hung up on Africa, world someone has gone to Africa, for a few weeks or so, and come back, and told you just how nice they was treated by the African people. Then the African came here to America, and told their side of story and we go all out for it. What I am trying to say that there are millions of people that have never set foot on Africa, so please don't be foolish; because if you are a V.I.P. there is someone to meet you at Nairobi, Airport in Nairobi, or Port Retz Airport in Mombasa in a bur or taxi to take you to a nice hotel and everybody treats you nice. I mean the red carpet is really rolled out, but still you didn't stay there long enough to meet the real Bush Brothers, come back to the U.S.A and just upset things, just let me say to you we are in the best state in the world and when I say best you better believe it, it is the best. Tongue will never be able to utter words enough to say we are blessed by God.

African people don't know what it is to use scented soap. The kind of soap they use is called Key Soap there is another name they have for it, it is Panger Soap. In America we call it Octagon soap and you know good in well we don't bathe with that, we American don't buy such soap.

All I can hear are our people and back home well brothers and sisters let me tell you American is my home always was and always will be. I would just love for those people who are going to say that I am lying could at least stay six weeks in Africa free of charge.

These African people are tribal minded who believe soap will destroy their confidence. They are tribal minded from birth they will tell you this is our culture and we wouldn't have it no other way. Back a few pages I mention about tribal body marks there is also a tooth pulling at twelve years old, some tribes have three teeth pulled out at the bottom of the mouth both male and female. There is another tribal that have two teeth pulled out from the top of mouth so and so forth. Each tribal knows his or her tribe from bearing the same mark.

African people don't use toilet articles like we do, such as: toilet tissue, toothpaste, and soap like we do. Well I know you are wondering what do they use, nothing. Oh and about the teeth pulling this is done before the sun rise in the morning the father pulls the tooth with a pair of pliers and a pocket knife and puts salt in the wound to stop the flows of blood. Your father in America sends you to a doctor to get your tooth pulled if it hurts, but in their case the tooth don't hurt when you reach twelve years olds pop is going to pull your tooth whether you want it pull or not, because you don't have no say or wants. Africa is man's world.

American girl or boy don't have holes in their ears with a stick through the hole tied on top of their head and this make the ears long like cows ears. We don't have any board in our nose like a pig to stop him from rutting up the earth. I had one African man to tell me his father cut his ears at fifteen and put gron weights in the holes, so his ears could grow long, and he could keep them rolled up on top of his head at all time he told me he had to eat and sleep with this during day and night, he said until one night he was in such pain and his head was hurting him so bad until he took the gron weights out of his ears one night and stayed in his mud hut room a week until his head stop hurting he said although he was hungry and sick, but he knew better than to come out without that weight in his ears, because if his father had seen those ears and no weights in them he would cut them off, close up to his head.

If an African woman put a scratch on an African man she will go to jail for a long period of time. They will tell you woman means nothing man is important.

American children are trained to sit and eat at the table in America with a knife and fork. There are children in Africa who have never seen a table knife or fork of any kind. We lived on an Island surrounded by water in Mombasa Kenya, East Africa for a period of nineteen months. There was forty-three different tribes on the Island of Mombasa and each tribe speaks his or her mother's tongue Swahili, and others language. Some of them can and some cannot distinguished the tribal barrier is traffic, and some African specialized in all human speech. Now here in America some of us can't speak good English and it is the only mother's tongue some of us know. Even the African woman learns a language that the African man is not allowed to know if, there are any African women in the U.S.A. they can very well verify my statement.

My husband and I learn to speak a little Swahili from the African they will at first ask you do you know Swahili you say no they then will tell you I'll teach you Swahili, and you will be excited to learn so you can communicate with him and just as soon as he thinks you knows, how to tell him good morning and good evening in Swahili he will start to talk about you in another language, because he knows you understands Swahili very well and he will talk about you in a language you cannot understand.

Because even a small child four or five years old can speak four or five languages so it is impossible to keep up in speech with them, they are so far ahead of you when I say this I mean us, the American people in difference languages.

But we had to learn a little Swahili to cope with them day by day one reason is you have a servants to do all of your work, wash your clothes, wash your car, wash your dishes, cook your food, clean house. Food is Chavia-Kooker in Swahili, water is Omaji, let the food get hot Chakola-Kipate-Moto in Swahili Chi-Na-Kabhawa tea in Swahili is Chai-chupa, coffee is Swahili Chaova, a little child is Moto-Mdogo is Swahili, a bad man in Swahili Mzee-mbay here is coffee in another name meaning the same things in Swahili but spells different, coffee meaning Kahawa one word of their means so many things and spell the same sound the same in some words there are a slight different in the spelling but sound the same.

A small field means Shamba-dogo we say in English that is your business in Swahili it is your Shurii, Grandmother is BiBi, Lady, go to sleep go Lilii, the old man set by the door, Mzcc-Alikaa-Mlangoni. To read Kuingia—to write Kuandika—to put Koweka—to went—Kutaka to go—Kuanza—to go out—Kutoka to began—Kuanza to sit—or stay or stand—Kusinama you will notice just about all of their words ends with capital A. a friend is—Rafiki, father is BaBa, mother is MaMa as in our language, cow is Ngombe, gook is Mbuzi, sheep is Kondoo, Pit is Ngurawe. Horse is Faras, donkey is Punda, dog is Nnbwa, cat is Paka, foul is KUKU, duck is Bata, pigeon is Njawa, ion is Simba, Leopard is Chui to carry—Chukka. I shall go now Hapana, Ngoja-Kidogo. The food was good—Chakkula—Kilito sha. I'll go to Mombasa to see my child in Swahili Nacnda. Mombasa Kwa Mtoto-Wanbu. The woman, the woman has gone to the river Swahili, Wana-wake-wamewenda-Mtoni, he have gone to his field in Swahili, Amekwenda-Shamba. The children have gone to school in Swahili-Watote-Wamek-Wenda-Shule. I mention one word in there in Swahili it means more than one words you take it for granted the women have gone to the river and the children have gone to school means the same thing.

Greet the old man with respect in Swahili is Mwamkie-Mzee-Kwa-Heshiwa. I am going home in Swahili Nakwenda-wetu well let's talk about America for a little while. Well someone is going to say what inspired Mrs. Armstead to write well its make me not different about the critic I have broad shoulders Hi Hi.

There is plenty to write about and talk about and learn about. There was a friend of ours who drop in one day for a visit he have a son is Africa, he was a little disappointed in him being there the son is in an exchange student in this part of Africa, it is such a unpleasant Exchange not only in this part of Africa that is all over the African continent. Where he is going to school so I sit and listen to his story on how he sends money every month, with clothing, shoes and what nots. For seven or eight months he has been sending him the ebony Magazine, he said on page 30 in the book he would always place $8.00 on that page for pocket money for the son and the young man have until now to receive that money and those shoes and clothing. We told the father that his son would never receive the money and the clothing and shoes. Once the African find out you are sending money or something in his country that he can use the owner will never receive it. Nobody but your Bush Brother is taking it and saying that Negro have a rich father back in America, and he will not receive anything his father sends him now. They are not giving a hoot about your government and have his brother in the U.S.A. for an exchange.

Then his brother are getting a much better education here in the U.S.A then the Negro is getting in Africa, he just can't see that far and the Americans can't see that far either, but still we are lit up over something we don't know about and some people will hold you a stiff argument about what he or she knows.

Well into Swahili stand back or get back means, Opahanda-Opanhanda Milk is Muxwy, going to the store or market, Mee-Mee-duka-quanda. An automobile is called a Gottie anything on wheels or anything that runs on four wheels is a Gottie the car hood is a Bonnet in Swahili the trunk of the car is the Boot in Swahili, good morning in Swahili is Jambo good night is Quhala, don't hit me is Pika I Swahili come in sir is Hodi-hoodi, hello Mr. Joe, Jambo-Bwana, hello Mrs. Johns, Jambo-Mamsal, an elder person, Jambo-Mam-Mam if it is a woman it is a man Jambo Ba-Ba, if it is a child, Jambo-toto that is to recognized that age person. Shop any repair shop is a Funda shop we say gasoline Africa says Petrol which is the proper name for gasoline you can see when an Africa knows English he speaks it better then we Americans do.

Butter in Swahili Gee-Gee can mean many different things such as key, oil, or soap. Come her, Kuhpwa—or Kuhae. Chicken is Coo-Coo. We go on a vacation here in America in Africa you go on a Safari each bottle is a jug no matter how small it is, anything to that holds water or liquid is a jug.

Two thousands, fifteen years and in American we have the African is just two thousand years behind the U.S.A just fifteen years ago the Africans people just stop circumcising there in the last fifteen years and in America we have never had this type of thing not to my knowledge. A chief is in every village and every tribe believes in their chief inspector. The chief of police in East Africa is the only man carries a gun the others polices carry's a short hard stick that is what they arrest you with, you better not run if you do the police will hollow thief the on lookers will run you down the prisoner, catch him with bare hands or stone him to death.

On week end we would get into a discussion with the African and ask them would you like to live like us the American people? And cut all of the tribal tradition, they would tell us no it is our culture and we must keep it, it is a must. Give if you give an African something like meat or something of value he will take it to his witchdoctor to find out if it is fit for him to eat or use.

Witchdoctor whatsoever the witchdoctor tells him, he is not going beyond that. This witchdoctor have never been or even seen a school house it doesn't matter how you doctor an African he believe in Voo-Doo. If there are ten people in one family working to send this girl or boy off to school to educate him or her they will work very hard to see that this girl or boy is educated and when he or she finish school they will go to college. Everybody worked, and everybody who worked there fingers to the bones to educated this son or daughter or cousin or niece or nephew they will all stop work and set down on this college kid, and tell him or her we sent you to school to take care of your family and kin. You have a good job now and you must take care of us and the girl or boy are very pleased with it no (sweat).

American do we do this in American? And if your marries a doctor or school teacher or superintendent, first father picks out the wife or husband for the husband or wife neither one have a choice it is daddy's choice. There is a large fee that the lesser family will have to pay. What they call dowry, ten cows if you have then goats, sheep, chickens, coca-nuts trees, pigs, and money they say shillings of course that bride can cost you a great deal of money it can run up into big money. With this good job you even have to take care of a long distance cousin if he is in that tribe. In East Africa a man or woman will not marry another man or woman if it is not someone from his or her tribe period.

American here in America we will say he or she is making a good salary in Africa they say here she is making plenty shillings, 30 shillings in America money in East Africa for an African person the value of 30 shillings in American money the value is $5.50 which in America is just a sovereign before herein the U.S.A. there is no exchange for it so therefore it do not value here in America.

Shillings:

5 shillings is .70

10 shillings is 1.40

20 shillings is <u>2.80</u>

All add up to $4.90 in U.S.A. money in Africa that is enough money to feed four or five families and about thirty-five Indians. Someone wants to now well the way people in U.S.A. eats how can this be? Well they eat different in the east and less and things we don't even know about and things we haven't never seen or even heard of their vegetables are very much different from ours when they cook meat it is cut into bite size, about the size of a marble they skin there chicken like we skin a rabbit here in the good old

U.S.A. before they fry it they boil there banana eat them green all fruit is eaten half ripen. Their type of food is cheap and unheard of in America and they know nothing about our kind of living. The British White man have had the African man feel and believe that if he eat plenty he will be pot belly and also told him an African would look funny pot bellied all African walk light footed because being a servant he have to pull his shoes of at Bwanas door before entering the door. He is bare foot, and put on his rubber shoes to go outside. I am writing form my own eyes experience, because I had servants two weeks after we arrived on this Island.

My husband and I had only six different servants: our first servant name was Millon Koydza, our second servant was John Kmanza, our third servant was John Mosia, our fourth servant was Richard Kumrum, our fifth servant was Joseph Useph, our six servant was Peter Makuau well somebody is going to say gee why so many servants in nineteen months, well they will work their fingers off to start with for one or two days then after the first on second pay day he starts to complain about family troubles and lying sick have to get off to attend a funeral or have to go to a doctor or take care of some important business in which he don't have if he is working for American. He will clean the white woman and white man house for less pay and when it come to clean the Negroes house he resent you wanting to be clean he wants you to sit and live in dirt like him. I am talking from experiences in the apartment where we lived we was mixed both white and black neighbors from American. You had to pay him more and then he complained he wanted to be slick pretended he could work elsewhere for more shillings.

No matter how nice you were to them they could steal from you and not from the white neighbor. Then if he worked for about so long as three months he would come in late drunk and complaining of being tired and what have you and if you turned your back he is off and gone home with your work undone and when pay day comes around he wants you to pay him more shillings then he deserved, we would treat them nice pay them off and let him go.

They get drunk off what they call African Juice its name in Africa is Scchici—this is natural sap from the coconut tree that they get drunk off. They climb the coconut tree just like a monkey all the way to the top cut into the vein of the limb of the tree about sun rise tie a gourd bucket to the limb and let that bucket stay there until 6 o'clock in the evening, pour this sap into an old nasty wood barrel for a week until it gets sour and stinky and ready to sell they set on the road on street corners and sell it for 40 a bottle in African money, and you haven't seen nothing yet until you see a drunk African.

Each African man have his own coconuts trees if you owns (4) or (5) coconuts trees you are consider a big shot you is called Bwana-Cova which means big shot in America that is big shot there language that don't apply for all Africans. Men some of them don't own nothing and don't want nothing there is no fence, no line around these trees everybody knows everybody business and everybody knows that is Joe Blow trees and nobody is going near that property not to even look at a coconut let's on eat one and if you do live you're a son of gun (smile). These trees are given to the sons from their fathers if their father owns any trees they handed down from fathers to father to be a boy child he is lucky in that way the poor little girl always sold, the selling age starts at eight years old.

It is nothing for a sixty year old man to have bought an eight years old bride sometimes before she is fourteen years old she has 4 or 5 children. This husband is taking care of her family he have promised he will take care of her family believe me a promise is a promise in Africa it is a most exciting time at the birth of a girl child in Africa because she is born for sale. At eight she is ready for market a deal is a deal (smile) one of my servants Peter M. Bakua names his little ToTo after me so in the near future little Willie Beatrice M'Bakua will be up for sale what a shame.

Steal is one African steal from another he can get as much as six years for stealing his brother chicken and if a woman cut an African man with a knife she can get pertained for life in prison. The African man will tell you African is man world, because African woman means nothing in Africa in the eye sight of African man, because she is not important.

Divorce there is no divorce in Africa in East Africa, if a man has been married to a wife for twenty years or more and gets tired of her all he is to do is to go next hut select another bride and put her in the same hut with wife number one no sweat. They live happy every after in the same shamble if they put the husband will stroke them both and neither one better not raise her hand. They are not allowed to quarrel or have any misunderstanding no fuss no mess.

Other wives and is a month or two or three weeks if the husband feels that two wives are not enough he goes out and collected two or three more wives and nothing bad never happens because all wives are happy together then if he have children by all four or five wives that makes it much better.

Brotherly love and if this husband dies and he have a brother left behind this brother will marry all of his dead brother wives, so he can take care of his brothers family that is to keep them together so they won't stray you see in Africa what's good for me is good for my brother, that is Bush Brother way of feeling that is there deep sense of love. Soul brother of America, but a soul brother of America just can't see things this way he wants a whole hog or none Hi Hi.

Tribalism, if a member of some tribes dies each member of that tribe has to cut their hair off and shave their head before attending the funeral man, woman, girl and boy if not you can't go to funeral you better not be caught there with hair on your head if so you will be excluded from your tribe forever no one of that tribe will never recognized him again.

Picture talking, I shot pictures ask questions every day of my life in Africa, one day my servant little girl came running into my apartment, head was as ball as a cue I hadn't seen her in three weeks or more than last time I had seen her she had nice hair on her head at first I didn't recognize her so when I did catch my breath and turn to her father Joseph who was my servant in the kitchen washing dishes, I ask why was Marier hair was cut off and her head shaved. He told me that his mother-in-law had died and it is our custom to cut off the hair and shaving the head before going to the funeral. Because right away I thought the child had a rash or some kind of itch in the head to cause the head to be shaved, but I notice I didn't see a bump that was the reason for the hair being cut off. African name in

Swahili for hair is Veli. All of their holidays are very much different from ours they care nothing about Christmas, Easter, fourth of July, Thanksgiving Day and so on their important holiday is boxing day we would ask them why do they celebrate boxing day they will tell you they don't know what they are celebrating it for all we know it just boxing day.

I would ask them if there a great heavy weight champion of Kenya that got defeated on a certain day, is this why you'll celebrate boxing day they would say no Mamsai I would ask who is the champion fighter they would tell me the only one they ever heard of was Cassius Clay and Dick Robinson of New York in the U.S.A on that certain day everything is closed up tight every African is off on that day, if he is working for you on that day you must let him off because that is an important day and if you don't give him time off you can come in serious trouble with the Kenya government there you will be penalized and discharge from their country.

Christmas day, everything is wide open on Christmas day nobody pay no attention to Christmas day they will tell you very quick Christ died for the Americans people and not for us the African people then I would tell them God love them to, they would say no he never did nothing for us. All he did was for the American, White man and the American Negro then I would say who's breath do you breeze he

17

would say my own I would ask who give it to you he would turn and say my mother. I would ask well who give your mother her breath he would say her mother.

Believe them I would tell him the reason we are blessed because we believe in God we pray to God, we thank God for many, many blessings, we are God fearing people and that is why God bless American and we didn't do like you Africans people try to build a tower to heaven just to get into God's Business we American try to be clean and cleanest is next to Godliness But you just can't get through to him, then they would say all of the American is rich we Africans are poor people. You see he looks out for you American people and not for us. I said well we appreciate him that is why, what he had one for us we love him we serve him we worship him and he always looks out for us, we never interfered in his business, because his business is pass man finding out. Our trying to build a tower to heaven and help mixed language all or you scorn Christ that is why your luck is mixed up and you too.

Africa death, some Africans believe when they die and their family buried them that they are going to lie in the ground three weeks and then sprout like a bean and return to their tribe. Some say when they return they will have their wish to go any place that they wish some say they are not going to return to Africa one of my servants told me that he was going to return to Mosco and not to Africa, there native dance is the Pochumber they can do this type of dance all night long without stopping before we left t he was trying to learn the Chubby Checker Twist before we left. Just for the fun of it not that they cared anything for it, it was just to laugh at the American way of dancing, it is funny to them and their sure is funny to me. We American are so wrapped up and so much in love with out African brothers and sisters, and the African woman and man; girl or boy wants nothing to do with us. When I say us I mean the Negro people when an Africa call you brother or sister you better believe he or she is trying to use us when I was in Africa there was a team of college kids that came to Nairobi for some school activity from the U.S.A. I read about it in the African daily Nation Newspaper. They had a dance on the night of arrival for the kids from the U.S.A. so they interviewed them while they were drinking and dancing and feeling good, and one of the poor little Negroes girl said that she knew she had found her heritage when one African brother walked up and called her sister.

What she didn't know and couldn't understand she was in a strange land and this smart African was just pulling her leg. He knew what she wanted to do to her while in his country so he and the next Bush Brothers had a good laugh about her because, they had rolled out the side of the carpet she wanted to see when she arrived in Africa and it was bright shining red, and this is my heritage; and when the African comes to the United States to be educated with our money oh naturally they are in love with us until their departure for their country back home.

Just as soon as their feet hit their own soil it's a different thing altogether. They can't go back bathing, shaving and getting all pretty like he had to do and was told to do here in America, striating her hair like she learned to do here in the U.S.A. they have to return back doing whatsoever there tribal of way of doing before they came here to the U.S.A. there people will tell them don't bring that nigger way of doing here do like you was taught to do before you went to the U.S.A. or if not you know what will happen to you. I'm trying to make it so plain so someone might see, so now you can see he or she was living on a strain while here living in the U.S.A. he said a negro wants to live like a Mon-zono that's means like a white man, that is because you being black have nothing to do with your wanting to be like someone else. As a good able thinking human being makes you wants the better things in life you don't have to live in a mud hut just because you was born black.

They will tell you very proudly we are proud port black and for an African we wouldn't trade our culture for no one. We are proud of being just an African we love our way of life. This is our country nobody goes to America and come back to Africa and tells us how to live and he will tell it to his fellow in some real low down Swahili. It's just makes me sick to my stomach to hear someone in American get up on television and call themselves talking Swahili and teaching others Swahili. First can't no Negro or white, blue or red American teach Swahili unless he or she was born in some part of Africa, or carried there by someone about the age of three years old or older so kids don't let anybody fool you.

The African scorns the Negro but yet we worship them and he worships the white man. We don't sleep on no dirt floor here in America, that is some of the jealously of them but America can't see that the African live, eat, and sleep in dirt and he look down up on you because you don't do the same as he do.

Try and explain and when you explain this to them about yourself and the way of life of how to be clean he will scorn you for it. I keep mentioning that I have witness to everything I write, tongue pen, pencil paper or what have you never will tell it all, the good old U.S.A. spent eight thousand cold cash American dollars to educate just one Africa when he finish his education in the U.S.A. and returned to Kenya while we was there he came back complaining angry and arguing with us about we were there in his country dodging the killing that was going on in the United States and the U.S.A. was real rotten and if it was left up to him he would blow it off the map, and it was his wish to take every American out in the African bush and make him drink blood or set everybody in American on a six foot ant pile.

He talked about America Negroes really pretty in Swahili. And this is what gripes me the big people go and come back from Africa, can tell you how nice he was treated you know why he was a V.I.P. of course when he mounted the soil in Africa the red carpet was rolled out for him cause he was treated with royalty, but this is what he fail to know he didn't see or mingle with the little follow at all because at the airport there was a limousine there to take him to this fabulous hotel owned and operated by the British people in Africa, and right away you being American you are brain washed straight away ad when the Africa comes to the U.S.A. he brain washes you all over again and again we Americans are soft hearted people and we are like a pecan in September we fall hard but as the old saying go if you don't stand for something you will fall for anything and you hang right in on what is being said.

Our kids in the United States of America and especially our kids and grown up here I America. They are really sold on it people who started this hair style the bush and the bush comb and afro, sheen hair pomade to keep the bush in shape well I hope nobody believes or think that is type of hair style come from Africa, because the African bush that is seen on many safari with the naked eye don't look like the one on the American people head by the way I didn't see no bush name hair in Africa and furthermore I didn't see no hair name bush there either.

The pars where the animals range and where people go on safari this is called out in the bush it is small, trees grows about five (5) feet tall and shaped at the top like an umbrella this is only in Africa not in the United States of America. There is all kinds of birds, zebra, lions, leopards, elephants, rhinoceros, hogs and all kinds of animals and when the Americans sees an African in his country with his or her cut or afro short, they just think it is a good style and I'm going to follow this it is way out and baby this is it and this thing just do something to me if some of these same people could see some of these slides and movies that we made of Fort Jesus where his good brothers the Africans seeing to it that the cause of his being sold it might wash off on somebody. The so called educated people are gone all out for it and plenty of them haven't ever been or never will go to Africa, Americans don't think for themselves and ask themselves questions why? Questions, you can feel some of the people some of the time, but you can't fool all of the people all of the time, and all

Africans are not poor people there are some rich Africans in Africa but he look down on the poor African brother like some of us do some of us. Sometimes there Africans people have just left a relative funeral and has to catch a plane for the United States of America on important business.

Oh it not going no place at all his or her hair would be short, because there is no means at all to take care of their hair, I'm talking about more than two thousand tribes they don't know what grease is for the hair and if they did, they are too tight or too poor to buy it or her husband don't allowed her to use it simply because they don't want her to look like a Negro Woman.

I've them to tell me that all the American women who powder their face and paint their lips, and straighten their hair are just a good American Hoe. Their comb is a single pick with a handle the girl comb is a double wood pick and here3 in American we have duplet plastic combs. This is the way I see it for myself God blessed us with hair on our head and still we are not satisfy, that is not enough to look like we have found fault of that God given way. Sometimes I wonder what would the Lord have to do next to make us happy, its seems as if we are never satisfied with is way of doing, we are never pleased with our self at all.

I think he made us in his own image in shape, form and size in the way he wanted us to be on the other hand we are not satisfied with hair, clothes, cars and sex. You name it in my book woman is man glory her hair is her glory once she gets rid of her beauty, so what do she have to offer? I think it would be an awful sight for my head to be bald and my husband head is bald too, and so as many others women who have bald heads husband. My sakes you couldn't tell who was who, or maybe I'm a little old fashion but think my god I'm not bald headed. When I see long hair men, women, girls, and boys in Americans with their hair long and down on their necks and backs. I say straight way there goes a true loved, true born America that who appreciates the hair God give him.

There are ants hills in Africa they are as tall as any six foot man and taller. These ants won't bite any Africa but will eat an American, I was told by an Africa that some years ago there was a Negro caught in Africa, and was put atop one of those ant piles, and has remained there until the ants ate the flesh off the body to the bone. These are the largest ants in the world. They all migrate together some of them ride each other piggy back; sometimes you see them going somewhere. A whole block long it is kicks to stand and see a dirt dabber build his castle, it is so seldom that it rain in East Africa Kenya and when it do the dirt dabber be the gladness thing in Africa, he fly from one mud hole to another getting a little dab of dirt trying to hurry up and build his house before the mud gets hard again he build and build all day long that day until its gets dark for him to see and he must stop, he can't sleep with it on his mind or either he have worked so hard he gets its off his mind instead of returning to where he left off from the day before he is easy to forget. He just flies and flies around in circles. Never can find out where he left off the evening before. All at once he go to the mud and start building anywhere he never can get himself together to go back to the first place he will start anywhere on the ground and a tree anyplace and it is as flat as a soda cracker, simply because he is nervous and forgetful and just don't have the time.

Mundi rock is the tallest and longest rock in the world, and it is the most exciting thing in the whole world people come from all walks of life, all over the world to see and make movies of this great rock. Movie stars do a lot of filming there too we filmed this roc, had lunch on the rock and it was just exciting to me, this rock is in Tosaia National Park. This rock come from a volcano of earth it was a mountain that was gas filled with dirt get so hot and exploded and burned into char-coal, and these char-coals turns into solid rock. This rock was about one half mile wide and twenty miles long and it is a beautiful light pint rock.

Char-coal hauling, some African go to these volcanoes mountains and haul all of their coal by a hand cart for their cooking and barbecuing when you see an African coming down the road with his cart fill to the top it is called the African Express.

Parish dice, Africa is God parish dice on our greatest Safari in Africa was a trip to the crater Ngora-Gara Crater you have not been on a Safari until you go into the Ngora-Gora Crater it is unbelievable it will bring tears to your eyes to look and see the work of the almighty god. This crater is also a volcano of Earth that God seen fit to fix this crater like a soup bowl its round like a bowl and there are miles and miles of earth as far as you can see all around you, and animals of all kinds are in this crater god planted small pine trees all around this crater so it won't decade in this crater there are thousands of animals down in this crater. This crater is seven thousand feet above man the animals never attempted to come out of the crater there are all kinds of animals living and laying down together just like you raise a dog and cat together here in the United States of America and they learn to love each other. The animals are zebras, impalas, lions, leopards, wild dogs, wilder beast, birds of all kind, beasts of all kind or any king there are plenty of little ticks, birds on each animal back and his head in his ears on his sides and legs. Keeping the animals free of tics and lice, there are plenty of food, grass and water the whole year round to feast on. They are eating, playing and happy the lamb and lions lying down together. God has them under his command they get along better then a big family of people it is just a miracle you couldn't never go in the guide its takes a four wheel drive to get down into the crater, and can't nobody drive or carry you down into the crater, but an African Chap as the British would call him. Because he can tell you just how close you can go to film the animals, you can't get out of the truck to film the animals you have to film them from the four wheel land rover. Filming crazy, we went crazy filming making slides and making movies of all these beautiful animals in Kenya.

T Savo National Park where we had our first Safari it is the largest park in the world, it is eight thousand, twenty-four miles of bush and occasional hills on the plains east of the tallest mountain in Kenya, Mt. Kilimanjaro is mostly two thousand and four thousand feet up divided into two sections east and west by the Nairobi Mombasa. Roads noted of great herds of elephants and hippos at Mt. Zima springs, opened all year unless rain makes the road impossible three lodges and two hotels at the gates of the T Savo National Park cover a vast section of the two hundred miles of Thorn Scrubie spiced with the bulbous trunks or boa bob trees that separates the tropical vegetation of the coast from the great central.

African continent, plateau of the continent, it was the endless thorn scrubi here that keep the people of the interior remote from western civilization for so many centuries. Try walking through it as the early missionaries did and you will soon understand it has various name the Nyira which means thorn country. The Nyiri, desert, the Taru much of the year it is burnt dry and dusty on the sun.

Then overnight the rain transfer mildew it convolvulus flowers burst out white and purple grass explorers hated if for the very reasoning that makes it a major attraction today. The game full of wild beasts such as rhinoceros, buffalos and elephants the German missionary Rebmann noted in his on May 11th, 1848 indeed it is full T Savo Park has the greatest concentration on elephant in the world. They are fairly accustomed to human beings now, though if you meet one on the road drives very cautiously, angry elephants are the natural allies of automobile scrap merchants. I will give you only a few names of animals the Africans elephant in Swahili is Ndovu—or Tembo is larger than the Indian particularly its ears. A bull weighs up to six (6) tons and stands twelve feet at the shoulder. The heaviest recorded single tusk from Tanzania reached two hundred and twenty-eight pounds. Elephants are intelligent live in herds and are vegetarians they inhabit both the bush and the mountain forest their life span is about 60 years I was told,

The hippopotamus its Swahili name is Kiboko, who name is Latin for river house is really of the pig family. Hippos congregate in schools and spends most of the day submerged in water up to the nostrils they came ashore to feed on grass at night a grown hippo weighs 2 ½ tons yet can outrun a man, male hippos fight each other to death.

The African Black Buffalo its name in Swahili is Nyati or Mbogo have been force to live in the forests and thick bush by approaching civilization despite its basic food being grass buffalo stay in herds and though shy are one of the most dangerous big game animals, a grown bull will weigh one thousand and five hundred pounds and the span of its horns maybe fifty inches long.

The black rhinoceros in Swahili he is Faru, weigh over a ton and is a solitary it have poor sight but good smell and hearing, although a vegetarian it is, it has tempered and will charge anything even a train. The rare white rhino is larger and better tempered but, not white its name derives from the Dutch word meaning wide, which refers to its distinctive square jaw the rhinos horn are composed of tightly paced hair not real horn.

The giraffe the Swahili name is Twiga the tallest mammal grows to eight feet and weights a half ton if browses on leave, especially

Acacia like open country and is in offensive its small horn and could in skin and soft hair the rectangular giraffe is so called because its making are square within a network of whitish lines instead of star shaped.

The common Zebra its Swahili names is Punda-Milia is found in open country over most of East Africa always manages to look sleek and well fed. Zebra moves in herds often with giraffe, eland and other animals they feed on grass, leaves and if necessary shrubs. A male zebra stands five feet high at the shoulder and weighs seven hundred pounds, the grey zebra is taller and has larger ears and narrower striped.

The greatest Mr. Lion the Swahili name is samba, it is found in open country throughout East Africa a full growth male weighs four hundred to five hundred pounds, the lions has no mane pride of families, he doze in the shade, during the day and hunt at dusk springing on the backs of the zebra, buffalos, and wilder beasts or whatever they have stalked they kill only when hungry once in three or four days.

Scat cat the long leopard, its Swahili name is Chui. He hunts by night is wary and extremely danger when hunted or cornered it makes its lair in cliffs or among rocks in thick bush its favorite food is balloon, although if hunger it will eats rodents and even insects. A grown male weighs under one hundred and fifty pounds and measures about seven and one half feet from nose to tail.

Here menny menny the eat its Swahili name is Mondo is short tailed, long legged and spotted with large ears, it look like a cross between a small leopard and a Iyna and it hunts at night feeding on birds and small mammals the several exists in many parts of East Africa, particularly liking places that are marshy and near water.

The cat cheetah the meanest cat ever lived his Swahili name is Duma look like a leopard and with longer legs and a small head. Also its spots are isolated not grouped in a pattern it hunts by day and is the fastest mammal in the world. It has been time at sixty miles per hour. Cheater stands three feet at the shoulder and is about seven feet long. They are easily tamed and have been raced against grey hounds in Europe.

The Wort Hog its Swahili name is Ngiri and it is named after the warts on its grotesque head. It lives on the plains in families or sounders and breeds in holes. During the day it crops grass or digs for roots with its tusks, while kneeling on its fore legs. It is related to the giant forest hog largest of the African Pig's which weighs over three hundred pounds and keep his tail high up in the air when he is running or about to move off. There are horns and knots on his face he is a real hog except for that. The African tells me they are good to eat they say it is rich and a sweet meat.

The spotted Hyenena its Swahili name is Fisi is a night time scavenger though its jaws can crush horn it is a coward and only attacks weak or aged animals, its color is yellowish and it weights about one hundred and fifty pounds. Hyanema have a characteristic unpleasant howl and they launch when lions are around. There is a striped species in North east Ugander.

The baboon its Swahili name is Nyani-Mkubwa is the large dog faced monkey seen in many parts of East Africa lives on the ground usually moving in troops under the leadership of a big old male and goes into the trees to sleep at night. Baboons will eat particularly anything, animals or vegetables the babies ride on their mothers backs. The Palas monkey its Swahili name id Kima rooms in troops of ten or twelve like the baboon it normally stays on the ground, using low trees or ant hill as observations points, its habitat is the dry savannah or North West Kenya, Tantania and Northern Uganda, in color it is reddish with white under parts and white side shickers on its face. The prettiest thing that I ever seen in East Africa Kenya, was the bush baby the little tiny monkey it Swahili name is Komba is a nocturnal relative of the monkey which lives mainly in Acocia

Bush. During the night you often see its large eyes winking at you out of the darkness. It is very active climbing and making tremendous, leaps in search of insect and quite during the day its sleeps whole families cuddle together in hollows trees trunks.

Grant Gazelle its Swahili name is Swala-Tomi better known as Tommy is more reddish in color then the Grants Gazelle which otherwise it is like, and had a distinctive blank band running alone its flanks it also has a habit of switching its small tail, the Tommy lives in large herds on the plains.

The common water buck its Swahili name is Juro it is a large antelope found in eastern Kenya and Tanzania, usually near water. A bull may lead a herd up to thirty cows, who have no horns, their coats are shaggy grayish brown and with a white rings on the rump. The Defassa waterbuck of Uganda has a round white patch instead of a ring.

The Sable Antelope the Swahili name is Palahala—or Mbaba-Pi is a splendid animal standing nearly five feet high almost black and bearing great scimitar shaped horns it is white on the under parts rump, and face in East Africa it is only found in a few coastal areas of Tanzania, and near Mombasa and likes lightly wooded country, it stayed in small herds.

Cokes Haslebceste, usually known as the Kongoni in Swahili is widely distributed in East Africa, its stays in large herds, grazing while one animal act as sentinel,, when surprised it snorts stamps a fore leg and gallops away, its color is light tan, bracket shaped horns and steeply sloping hindquarters make it easily recognizable. The wilder beasts its Swahili name for it is Gna-Or-Nyumbu are seen in vast herds migrating across the Serengeti Plains every year is one of the commonest antelopes I open country all over East Africa, it has a dark gray body, a white beard, a shaggy mane, and a clumsy gait horns look slightly like a buffalos it stands about five feet at the shoulder.

The Eland is the largest of the antelope and it Swahili name is Pofu-or-Mbunsa, often along sided zebra and giraffe they are often in open counter over most of East Africa. Both sexes carry heavy twisted horns a full grown bull weighs over one thousand and fifty pounds and stands six feet high at the shoulder there color is grayish brown, with lights stripes.

The Impala Swahili name is Swalap-Ala is a tiny medium sized Antelope famous for leaping in the air when alarmed it can jump thirty feet and rise ten feet above the ground impala moves in large herds they have smooth chestnut colored coats and tufts of black

35

hair on the hind legs above the hooves only the male carry horns found in Acaia bush and scrub country.

The great Kudu it Swahili name is Kandala-or-Kubwas, like rockie and mountains bush a male stands five feet high at the shoulder and weight about six hundred pounds. The female has no horns Kudus bodies are a lavender gray color white stripes the lesser Kudu-Kandala-Ndogo is rather smaller and has no fringy of hair running down its throat it lives in thick bush and scrub.

The Uganda Kob, of Uganda and North West Kenya, stand three feet high at the shoulder it has a sleek red gold coast with white under parts and white ring round the eyes the Kob, drinks daily so it is never far from water it stays in herds and the male fights savagely to master their harems.

The Puku of southern Tanzania is a large animal of the same genus. The Oryx it Swahili name is Chokoa one of the most handsome powerful and fierce antelope, is found in varying species from Ethiopia to Kalahari, it is reddish brown in color with black and white face markings. The female grows longer horns that the male up to forty inches. Oryx stand four feet height at the shoulder and weighs up to four hundred and fifty pounds. They move in small herds. Ambosel and Tsavo are good places to look for them.

The Gerenum, or Walter Gazelle its Swahili name is Swala-Twga has a delicately income grows long neck and the Giraffe like head it is a dark rough color. Roler on the flanks and white, white band over its eyes stands 36 to forty one inches high at the shoulder and weighs about one hundred pounds only the male has horns gerenuk wanders in small groups browsing on leaves in Acacia throw country.

The Dikidik its Swahili name is Suguya stands only fifteen inches high and weighs only twelve pounds. It lives in driest thorn scrub and is usually seen in pairs in color it is gray or grizzled brown has a shaggy coat and a distinctively long nose.

The Klipspringer is in many ways similar but larger standing about twenty-one inches high at the shoulder.

The Bongo same name in Swahili is the largest of the forest antelope though smaller then and eland. It stands four feet high at the shoulder and both sexes carry horns its color is a bright reddish chestnut with vertical with stripes. Bongo lives only in mountains, forest and are very shy and seldom seen.

The Bush buck its Swahili name is Mbawala or Pongo is a beautiful marked small animal with a white underside to its tail it prefers forest and thickets to open country, and sky also it lives in families not herds, a male stands three feet high at the shoulder and weighs about one hundred pounds.

The Sitatunganzohi is a swamp dwelling variant of the same species. The Colobus Monkey its Swahili name is Mbega, often called the same is jet black in color with a magnificent white mantle round its back, a white face and a white tipped bushy tail. It lives in highland forests like the Aberdares of Kenya eats leaves and very rarely descends from the trees.

The Sykes monkey its Swahili name is dark blue gray, in color with black fore limbs hands feet crown of head and tip of tail. It eats fruit and greenery and inhabits forests near water, it is known for its friendliness others variants of the species are called silver and golden monkey from the coloring.

The Chimpanzee the Swahili name is Soe-or-Mtu the most intelligent of the Ugander and Western Tanzania. Chimpanzees are small and are wonderful acrobats they lives in family parties of twelve or more. Chatter, noisily and are vegetarians although they take occasional bird eggs.

The mountain Gorilla its Swahili name is Sokwe is the largest of Apes, sharing with man the lack of a tail a few groups inhabit the forest of south West Uganda, they lives off wild celery and bamboo shoots, move on all four feet and sleep in nests, a male weighs about four hundred and twenty pounds despite their great strength gorillas are peaceful by nature.

The Secretary Bird the proudest bird in the world so called of its sedate strutting walk, and the quick like feather on its neck is often seen in East Africa, although it can fly alright it kills snakes, lizards and mice for food by striking them with its feet. Its wings are grey and black and it has a distinctive orange-yellow patch round its eyes, it's a large bird nearly thirty inches high.

The ostrich one of the great attraction of East Africa, it cannot fly, but has a kick that will kill a man. And can run at 45 miles per hour fully speed. A full grown Ostrich it can be eight feet it lays eggs in clutches of fourteen or more you often see it on the plains among herds of animals, true to some stories it does sometime hides it head on the ground when approached.

As well as the wild life Kenya is home to more than 48 Africans Tribes some like the Masia are famous as hunters and warriors, Rudolf for the Walingule elephant hunters, near Tsavo parks are few in numbers. Shy and still backward, the largest are the Kiluyu (2,000,000) whose homestead are between Nairobi and Nylri the Lou, (1,750,000) of the Kisumu area of Lake Victoria, the Kamba center of Machakso and Kitul and the Kalenjin of Western Kenya. The total Kenya African population is over ten million a century age thee was great rivalry between the tribes, but today everything is concentrated on collaboration and Kenya motto is Harmbee which means let's all pull together.

Nonetheless tribal dances and costumes are cherished as part of the country cultural heritage they are brimful of vitality too and the emu drummers for instance have drawn crowds to over sees performances in London and elsewhere. Broadly there are two ways of getting to see some tribes dance first if there is a celebration on such as Independence Day, December 12th there are likely to be public performance, secondly if you are on tour you may find an exhibition arranged at some point, for instance there are displays everyday: at the Mount Kenya Safari Club. If you want one arranged specially then most tribes are agreeable and a travel agent should be able to fix it for you the cost may however, be up to one thousand shillings in Kenya money it is not much in value as you would think of a thousand dollars in American but one thousand shilling in Africa money is just one hundred and forty dollars in America money. A word of warning here if you happen accidentally upon a local Ngoma, which is Swahili for a dance or celebration make sure to ask if you may stay and watch especially before taking photographs.

These are private affairs Africans is one of the beautiful places and sights in the whole wide world, every picture is a good picture and a more colorful picture, but no but wants you to take a picture, I have one of my servants to tell me I was taking his picture to carry back to the United States to sell and make money off it he went on to say just how poor he was still going to be and just how rich I was going to get for selling his pictures. Well I have too much pride to tell you in this book of what I told him in person so it goes to sure you a book don't tell (smile) for instance I finally broke it down to him told his that nobody in the United States of America wants to see your picture not speaking about buying it John I just want a picture of you to have to remember you by. But poor John couldn't understand.

When the British colonized and developed East Africa, they introduced both Asian and European minorities the Asians came mostly to work on the rails way then branched into trade today there are over 200,000 of them mostly in the cities and you will notice their masques temples and bazaars the silk turbans and the women's brightly colored saris however many are leaving to live in Britain or returning to India and Pakistan.

The European settlers are progressively being replaced by whom the country rightly belong to the Africans, farmers though a vast settlement scheme covering four million acres mostly in the highlands, however there influence remains evident in various ways, like having many open air craft despite the glorious climate.

Independence Day was on December 12th, 1963 and a year later Kenya became a republic in the common wealth under the presidency of Jommo Kenyatta. The national assembly sits in Nairobi administratively Kenya is divided into provinces the coast Fill-Vally central, western, eastern and north eastern climate.

The pleasant climate has had a lot to do with Nairobi booming success being 5,500 feet up the nights and cool while during the day the sun is warm but the humidity low. The temperature rarely exceeds 80%.

The main shopping street are Kenyatta Avenue intersecting Kimathi Street round the Bazoor are a multitude of Asian shops some selling curios silk saris and silver work if you want to see the rough hurly burley of African markets go down the river towards pumwani in central Nairobi some shops marked up the price when tourist come into view at times it may be advisable to bargain it is doubt consult the information at bureau at the queen way and of Kimathi Street.

Elephant hair bracelets are an East African lucky charm often worn by hunters. The new Stanly Hotel and restaurant is the city charm of Nairobi. Africa the capital of Mombasa, acknowledge social rendezvous during the day and a stimulating mix up of diplomat film stores on Safari looking dressed to kill in all senses of the world.

Near Kiambu and Thika there are coffee and sisal estates easily visited by arrangement but great interest lies in the KiKu Yu village a family may occupy there on more of the traditional round thatches huts though increasingly they are being replaced by more modern rectangular houses both land and firewood are in short supply which in why cattle graze on the road verges and you may see women pass by caring loads of wood, brought from traders held on their back by a traditional leather thong passing round the forehead. Kikuyu woman do much of the work on the family plots of land. Shamba in Swahili and some men have several wives, however, the Kikuyu are one of the most forward looking tribe in Africa, and female's emancipation is on the way Jomo-Kenyatta Kenya's president is a Kikuyu the Kamba-Masial-Amboscli reserve.

Most of the Mombasa roads 307 miles are now Tasmac and the rest is rapidly being improved from Nsirobi it leads out southeast past the National Parks and on the Athi plains it then skirts Kitui the Kamba are Kenya third largest tribe lie being soldiers, and are noted for their wood carving and there spectacular dancing, spiced with fantastic gyrating leaps in the air double sommer south.

Barely speaking the Kamba lives north of the road and the Masai South indeed Masia land. Stretches from Nairobi to Tanzania the frontier divides the tribe and westward to a legendary warrior tradition the young moron or warrior. Athletic aquiline featured his hair braided and thickened, with red ochre looks like a figure off a classical Greek vase as he stands leaning on his spear. His traditional stories are folk epics of lion hunts and he grows up believing that they are told only at night because, if you waste time telling stories doing the day you will go blind like the Tuioma moran he lives by and for his calls.

The traditional Masai food is blood mixed with milk and curdley, the blood itself being expertly taken from a view in a cow's neck without injury to the beast. Most Masai still live nomadically building their Manyatta, wherever there is graying a Manyattas is a group of low huts made of mud and cow dung and surrounded by a thorn fence inside which the cattle are brought at night for protections, you see them everywhere in Masai land of ten abandoned because, the herdsman have move on to new pastors.

The Mombasa road beyond Amboseli lays mount ilimanjaro. Described under Tanzania as the section is on Kenya we will return briefly to the Mombasa road the condition of which used to be a piece of national folk lore, but which has been so enormously improved since independence that nowadays there is nothing but praise for it like other roads in East Africa it has mileage boards marked with abbreviations of place names thus stands for Mombasa and Nbi for Nairobi the less tiring way, between the two cities is still by aid or on the comfortable overnight train the old town.

The most fascinating part of Mombasa is the old town that lies between Mak adora Road and the harbor its narrow between streets are overshadowed by high houses with elaborately carved ornamental balconies itinerant.

The Arabs sell coffee from traditional long headed cooper pots; oriental music drifts out from the shops of money lenders gold smith tin smiths, tailors makes of sweet meats and other traders.

Mostly Asian oriental mosques and temples like the new Jain Temple, its pillars ad domes as white as icing on a Gargantuan wedding cake.

Jostle for space with bustling African markets and stalls. Everywhere there is hustle life and a multitude of language Mombasa in fact has the same cosmopolitan feeling as Hong Kong, Singapore and others world parts both old and new parts deserve a visit.

At the north corner of old town stands the Portuguese castle. Fort Jesus weathered and immense its building began in 1593. Later the Arabs took it after a 33 months siege through they lost it again briefly, today its guns still command the harbor looking out beyond English point but the Fort itself houses a comprehensive museum dealing with the culture architecture and history of the cost of Fort Jesus. Fort Jesus is open daily and a detailed booklet about it is on sale at the entrance beneath the battlements a path leads along the shore where you can watch local fisherman casting their nets and giant Iguana-Lizards.

Scutting among the rocks, this path is one of the best places to photograph the Forth which is not an easy subject. You can photograph all day long at Fort Jesus the Museum s so large you never could take pictures of everything, that is, where the Arabs sold the black man to the white man and shipped him to the United States of America thank god. He did, what a change was made, just to visit there will give you the creeps to see those tiny little cells, where slaves were kept and put to death, so I am told in 1963 December 12th when Kenya received her independence the stone post that weighed about one thousand pounds where the Buyers and Traders would tie up their boats, and ships to await the arrival of the Arabs to bring the slaves out for sale. After your good African brother caught and brought you out to the ship there you would be bided on stripped naked and weighed, turned around and around and then sold the bid was off, so the day of December 12th, 1963 the pole toppled and fell to the bottom of the Indian Ocean.

The rest of Mombasa is a modern thriving city basin its prosperity of Kilindine harbor one of the main shopping streets in Kilindini road leading to the port post close round Salem Road, and Nyirere Avenue a visit to the African market in Mnembe Tayari, off Kenyatta and beaded hats there not to mention all the necessary herbs and relics for which doctoring more conventional medicine and photographic goods can be had from the central pharmacy in Kilindini Road the best Hotel on Mombasa island is the O'Ceanic a mile from the centre with swimming pool and dancing nightly in an air condition restaurant it charger about ninety shillings per day; also provides free transportation to its one beach at Bamburi the other seen hotels in Mombasa itself mostly have air condition bedrooms and are convenient, but none have a decent beach of its own for this reasoning there is much to recommend the various beaches, hotels on the mainland North and south of Mombasa Island though in Mombasa district which extend in both directions.

The Nyali-Beach-Hotel four miles north across Nyali toll bridges is first class has open air, dancing and a bar on the beach. It runs its own buses to Mombasa and meets trains eight miles north there are white sands at Bamburi the Dolpine at Shanzu and the whispering palms at Kikambila-Nyali incidentally has a good golf course, (the other is on the Island close to the ocean) to the south across the Likoni-Ferry is the Shelly-Beach-Hotel charge run from 451 shillings to 901` shillings a day with meals at all these hotels.

For eating in towns there are restaurants and night clubs, the Sala Bowl in Kilindini road specialized in seafood. The Hong Kong restaurant in Chinese food and the Bella Vesta serves good food. Above all the Oceanic and Nyali beach can be relied on for an excellent dinner the Oceanic Grill room has a night club atmosphere although it is more night life there then in Nairobi it's a matter of taking the rough with the smooth.

The little theatre club provides a good evening of entertainment temporary, membership is available to visitors. The New Florida in MaMa Ngina-Drive is above the only night club you can spend a sailor night out at the Star Bar or the Rainbow Bar. MaMa NyGina Drive is a short name in honor of president JoMo-Kenyatta Wife.

For sightseeing Mombasa taxis have a Legal Tariff of 20 shillings an hour and for shorter journey ought to charge by the meter local tours agencies such as Dalgety and company (box 30) floods tours box 2 28 and Mitchell Cotts Box 141 alternatively they or the African Roadways in Kilindini Road can provide self driving cars at around

3% shillings a day, plus Shsll a mile the air chart company operation from Port Reitz Airport is Wilkin air services north of Mombasa.

To reach Kilifi and Malindi you drive out over Nyali Brigge where the old Portuguese harbor light tours still stand and turn left past Freretown. This was a church missionary society settlement of freed slaves whose descendants run their old church Mombasa was a great centre for missionary work and there is a handsome memorial to Dr. Kraff on English point, beyond the bridge over the MtWaPa river is the turning to the KiKambala beach hotel. Further on ten miles from Mombasa on shawzu bay is the Dolphine Hotel Box 1443 Mombasa which charge from Shs 551 bed and breakfast this is all Giriama country and in the valley you can see the Giriama women who wear short white flowering skirts with vast bustles of coconut fiber underneath. At Kilifi 36 miles from Mombasa is the Marani club, a big game fishing club with its own air strip gray and facilities for water skiing sailing, goggling, aqua lune diving, underwater photography as well as fishing, charges about Shs 70% a day with meal and Shs 71 50 daily for temporary membership from Kilifi ferry to Malindi is an hour drive. Giriama-womens-hair dressing. These Giriama women dress there haired with red clay it is a sight to see they take the hair into their hands and red mud and roll the mud into their hair in tiny little rolls. Malinda is a tours attraction Malind is a totally delightful small resort it has pretty near everything one could want a few. Arab runs a few shops an attractive villages and a real beach coming atmosphere they bay runs in wide sweep of glorious sand on which a break in the reef lets the rollers in but not the sharks so you can surf wide.

There are four good hotels, the most sophisticated being the bin bad which has a resident ladies hair dresser don't thinking of hairdressing as we American do these hair dressers on Saturday evening Lowfards is a band type of beach and hotel very relaxed.

The other two are the Blue Marlin and the Eden Roc. The only one with a swimming pool. A couple of miles out is the drift wood club cheap with simple chalets dancing under the moon and a fleet of small boats for serious fishing Malindi has fine ferns. Most notably H. B. Swan Box 70 and "V" Boats LTD. (Box 131) during November there are fishing contest as part of the Annual Malindi Sea Festival, while in February when the Martin and Sailfish are running the International Bill-Fish competition takes place with participants from all over the world

It hardly needs saying that you want to book in advance in the Hotel you can fly EAA from Nairobi to Mombasa or use the happy taxi that operate a car, twice a day each way between Malindi and

Mombasa at a fare of 33/Shs. For local tours consult Sea Sun and Game Safaris (Box 64 Malindi telephone 57).

The Rift Valley, the first sight of the great rift valley itself will remain with us forever. Suddenly you come out of a thin belt of forest, round a corner and there two thousand feet below you down a sheer escapement is the rift quite literally the greatest valley in the world. It's floor is tanny Red in the drought or a dusty green the rains thirty miles away its further wall rises dark purple against the blue sky. A procession of clouds drifting across its peaks straight ahead stands the clear cut cone of longonot, 9,111 feet high, deep in whose crater you can see wisps of stem dying up among the trees. Dozens of volcanoes erupted in the Rift. The greatest being Kiluanjaro almost all are now extinct the reasoning was that the valley is the result of two roughly parallel faults in the earth surface; between which in an age before history. The land subsides and the earth crust was weakened.

The rift stretches from Lake Baikeal in Russia, down through the Lebanon and the Red Sea to Rhodesia in Kenya it holds Lake Rudolf Baringo Hannington, Nakuru, Nawasha, and Magadi, a western branch of the rift from Lake Tanganajika and also Lake Albert, Edwards, and George.

He mountain among mountains a mountain in itself, a mountain that have, snow the year round, a mountain where the snow, never melt, Mount Kilimanjaro in Kenya East Africa.

Mount Kilimanjaro, many people are drawn by the magnificent and mystery of Africa highest mountain. Mount Kilimanjaro lying only there degrees, south of the equator yet crowned with a permanent ice cap often the only visible sign of the mountain is the great snow mantled shoulder of Kibo (19340 feet) thrusting through a ring of cloud, the lower slopes and forests are hidden. The root of Africa ranks among the highest volcanic mountains of the world consisting of three separate volcanoes of different ages which have been welded into one great mass covering an area 56 miles by 38 miles.

The oldest of these volcanoes known is Shira, (13,140 feet) is seven and a half miles to the East of Kibo while Mawenzi seventeen and a half mile to the East.

The Majestic dome of Kibo is the youngest of the volcanoes. The first European to see Kibo was Johanes Robman in 1848 and the first to reach its highest point, Hans Meyer in 1892 climbers now a day follow closely the route taken by most of the early explorers. They start from Marangu, which means many waters, where the

Kibo and Marangu from Mashi the Tariff at the Kibo Hotel is 60 shillings to 70 shillings per person full board and at the Maragu Hotel from shillings 60 full board.

Arusha Africa is an old trading post that is now the most important town in northern Tanzania, the administrative headquarter4s of its region and the place where president Nyerere, set out the famous "Arusha", in great north road halfway between Cairo and the cape is marked by a plaque near the new Arusha Hotel and it is also the exact geographical center of East Africa. Despite its recent rapid a growth it has managed to retain a pioneering air yet is paradoxically reminiscent of an English town in Mount Merff an extinct volcano like Kilimanjaro its avenues are ruotous with namdi flame trees and blue flowering Jacarandos, while brightly dressed Africans walks proudly though the busy street. Gathering in the markets where they will usually consent to be photographed for a small fee.

The largest Hotel is the New Arusha which as the advantage of a swimming pool in its own garden. A very welcome amenity after a day out in the bush traveling along dusty roads. It now has 135 bedrooms all with private bath, taiffe range from shillings 601 per person bed and breakfast.

The new Safari Hotel used to be famous. Immumerable photographs of game the Leopards skins Masai shields and spears and the long shining cooper bar top all created an intimate atmosphere in this famous bar.

From Manyara the road winds up the mountain side, thought beautiful and spectacular scenery to the nogorongore ceater 37 miles away the best of a conservation area that contains the greatest permanent concentration of wildlife in Africa in a setting of unequalled grandeur. Some 10,000 Masai live near Nogorongoro visitors can spend a day in the crater and see wilder beast and zebra in thousands, driving peaceful through the herds while the ngorongoro lions, and almost as famous as those of the neighboring Serengeti with luck and early morning visitor will see at least one lion, and his mate tearing at a kill of wilder beast or zebra with the attendant. Scavengers Hyena, Jackal, and vultures hovering hear by ngorongoro crater lodge sits on the lip of the crater it has a log style dining room lounge and bar. Most other buildings are of log construction their rural aspect contrasting strongly with the highest standard of comfort inside.

Warm clothing is advisable for early morning and evenings as the lodge is nearly 8,000 feet above sea level. The full day starts at 901 shillings per person, and booking should be made through your travel guide agents. A full day tour of the crater in a six seater land rover with an African guide costs 2001 shillings, the vehicle can be shared with other guests. The food you carry on your safari is cooked by a resort staff of African like fried chicken in Swahili Co-co or ham in Swahili Gama or boil eggs and etc.

One shillings .12 in American value 14 shillings is $100 in American value, count from their $250 is 14 shillings it is easy to count their money after you learn it, but it is hard as hell to even guess what it is before you learn a penny from a nickel and a quarter from fifty cent piece.

We want to be identify so bad here is some of the identification. I don't know if we will ever accept if after we thought we wanted it and when we find out what it is then I wonder if we will reconsider it or will it surprise, our wants from our foolish thoughts.

Well on one Sunday I picked up the Sunday paper nation newspaper in Africa and begin to read the problem of young Africans, young Arabs, young Indians, this once stuck in my mind it goes like this it is a strain looking after family or dead brother. I was the youngest of four children in our family and the only have an education my parent who are now dead made me marry two wives and I have children by both of them, my brother who had three wives, had died and left two widows and ten young children. My two sisters are now being divorced and have been told to repay all that was paid for the marriages. I love my brother's children and am paying their school fees but I cannot stand this life alone.

My brothers' widows help me house and feed these children. My salary is 800 shillings per month that is less then eighty dollars a month in U.S.A. money but, it is likely that in the next few years this is not going to be enough. How should make use of these illiterate women to educate my poor children? I am staying in the town of Mombasa and my poor widows stay 200 miles away. There production is only approximately food stuff for the children. Just answer this first question is this your thing in America well if this our bag just hang in.

All cut up about hair, I cut my hair short two years ago and it had not grown since I have tried using oil but this doesn't help my hair, also falling out what can I do? My guest is the person body, needs vitamins of some kind for the body.

Face the truth; will you kindly help men save my face? My name is J.B.M. African boy I talked to a certain very beautiful lady so well and with such good manners that in the long run she feel in love with me. Late I learned the lady is well educated and is working as a secretary. I am a poor boy with a mere primary certificate and unemployed, because of this I fear meeting her though I love her none the less what can I do. In American we know to do whatsoever we see first we know not to ask no question we know what to do.

These are some of the known facts about Africa. Now listen to this eighteen year old boy, better known as Chap in Africa by the British I am deeply in love with a girl of the same age. When I tell her I want to go live in Tanzana. She said she would did without me what kind of love is that.

This is an African girl about the same age: is there any harm in choosing a man 15 years older than me if so why do my people have against this but, I do not agree with them. There have been a bit of disagreement Mrs. Armstead now you know ain't no soul sister in America going to ask no such question like that.

Still a boy at 21, I'm a boy of 21 years of age and I'm doing my degree of medicine at Makerere. Four years ago my father had married a girl for me and has paid the doury at this time; I was so young I didn't know much about love affairs. When I went home on holiday my father wanted me and the illiterate girl to associate but, the girl is wrong for me according to my standard. When I refused to have sexual relations with her she went back to her parents. My father is very worried because, he can't pay for another one. I could go on and on in the book telling you of young and old Africans people telling me there testimony.

The dying aunt of president Jumo-Kellyettas, on her death bed an aunt of president Jumo Kenyettas leaves her wishes with the family she called them all to her bed side and say I have something to tell you all. All of my ToTo's means all of my children she summoned her three sons and most of her 200 old grandchildren to her hut. On one Friday night August 29th 1969 she told them, I'm dying and there shouldn't be no fuss about it, slaughter a goat to cleanse the house the goat should come from no other hut, but this one I bless you all. With these words Maria Wanjiku Kuwgu was her name she reported to be one hundred and twenty-years old passed away in the early hour of that same day.

The word is meaningless, the word tribe and its more recent derivative tribalism is used in Africa, by African with great frequency, but does not seem that any of them are quite clear what this piece of terminology really denotes. For example they fill in official from each day, and whenever they arrive at the paragraph which demands one tribe they never hesitate to write.

Kikuyu or Lul Ya or Luo, but can't no one tell with precision what these words signify, do they for instance refer to cluster of people bound together by a common blood heritage; or do they simply mean a group of people brought together by historical circumstance and, therefore speaking common languages and observing common practices and tabsos, that is to say is tribe simply a culture linguistic community, if they assume a tribe it is a community of common thing the tribe are immediately in trouble if so, some of them couldn't remain in the same tribe.

Most of its inhabitants trace their ancestors to Uganda, Busoga or Baluhyaie, Bantu, speaking regions of east Africa, it is possible to speak o Lula lood or Kikuyu blood it is impossible to say that the people in South and Central Ivanza, are all Luo. Previously speaking and that the people who live in the central and western province of Kenya are respectively all Kikuyu and Abaluhya if by these we mean blood connections.

Blood wise, most of the inhabitants of southern Kikuyu for instance are blood wise more Masai than they are Kikuyu although they generally pass under Kikuyu. Classification that the Kikuyu are now impure with other blood likewise the people of southern Buluehyre are no Luo or Baluhya because, of the intermarriage that has gone on for so long between the two, and the Tiriki (sometimes called Uyangori) are no more Baluha then they are Kalenjin) what about the Banyala? Are they Lucor-Luhyu?

Again if they take the other view that a tribe is a culturalcum linguistic organization, a few scruples may cross the mind for example the people who live around the Karrarapon and Ngong hill areas generally call themselves Masai but, although they have Masai blood in them they are so mixed with the Kikuyu, that many of their present customs are practically Kikuyu. In origin, and they get along well with the Kikuyu. Language brings me to the topic which inspired this article one week a letter appeared in the African local press grumbling that there is a tribe somewhere in south Nanza called Basuba which is not recognized officially as a tribe. Who are the Basuba? The word Basyba has been used to describe rather loosely, the people who live in the two Islands of the Kenya, parts of Lake Victoria Rusinga and Mfangano and of the adjacent south Nyanza mainland locations of Kaksingri-Gwassi and Suna and more recently in ports of Kasigunga and Lambue valley.

Ancestry, these people are now all Luo. Culturally and linguistically but, they do not seem to be Luo in origin there are clansman in Ruginga Island trace their ancestry to Bugandfa. The trouble is in Africa he never wrote history or kept record of nothing. For example, you ask a mother how old is her child? She will tell you she don't know you have to ask the father. The people came from Buganda only doing the last century. The late Mr.Tom M'Boya clan Kamasengre of Rusinga. There is a sub-clan as Wamwamga ow professor Ogot assers that the people of Kaksingr came as refugees during a court revellion avainst Kabaka-Mwanga or Burganda. Does Wamwanga in Rusings mean that people of Mwanga where they breakway group from Kaksiongr.

The inhabitants of Gwassi however appear to have come from Kisii and therefore, ultimately from Maragoli in Buluhya while those of Scnac and Mohururu seem to be off shoots of the Kuria of Batende o the Tanzania border. The Aatende according to the Kisii and are also thus originally Maragoli. An interesting pointing one might see with regards to the people of Gwassi is the name itself it is said to be no more than a corruption of the word Gussic as the Kissi people call themselves the Mfangano islanders seems to be related to the Bantu speaking people of Ukerewe and Sesse Islands respectively in Tanzania and Ughanda. Linguistically they have undergone the last Luo influence still speaking Luo with unmistakable Bantu habit. Such as adding vowels at the end of words where such vowels do not exist in the Luo words, "Ochiengi for example is the same as Ochieng only things one word have an ending with an I and the other don't. but culturally they are all the people of PinJe-Abich the five lands as the Basuga organizationally call their location are totally Luo.

In Gwasi and Suna and Mohuru they have all dropped the younger Bantu to use 19th century European, anthropological term custom of circumcision, in rusinga Mfangano and Kaksingri no such thing was necessary the Baganda who are their ancestors do not circumcise will extract six lower incisors is enjoyed by the Kenya Luo. Although nowadays this custom of yet unknown origin is getting discarded more and more throughout Nyanza. Some of the later and younger generation have all of there god given teeth the people of PinJe-Abich which is a small tribe also observe all the Luo, practices and taboos' connected for instance fishing seasonal. Marriage and succession rites but, although most of these people speak Luo as perfectly as anybody from GenSakawakarachuonyo-or Kisumo this the way it should be written when it refers to the location for Kisumu, was as European corruption who are suppose to be the proper Luo.

They are unique in the sense that they have not dropped the Bantu language they has brought with them they are bulinguai. My father, father four fathers speaks Lusuba as effectively as he speak Luo, that is why these people now call themselves Luoabasuba if they are mixed blood wise and if thought the use of Lusuba they still retain elements of their for most Bantu, cultures it is good for them.

Their extra blood and culture-linguistic assets cannot fail to be the factor behind their industry, enterprise and genius cultural and blood hybrids. I have often found they have vitality above ordinary but, as I say the Luo, impact on them is indelible now indeed they militantly claim to be as Luo; as anybody I cannot see anything the matter with it as the correspondent referred to above seems to. I disagree with the social anthropologist-Okot-Pbitek who claims that the Lango o Uganda are not Luo.

Okot assumes the dangerous attitude, that the Ango president Obote's people being serologically related to the Teso and Karamojong of Uganda and not Luo. Kalenjin and Masi of Kenya and not Luo. That is they have no genetical connection with such proper Luo, as the Acholi (Okot's people) and the pad hole of Uganda the Alur of Uganda and Congo and the shilluk of southern Sudan. But, to me the Lango are as Luo, as Luo, can be all their customs are Luo in origin and the Kenya Luo will probably understand a Lango better then he will understand an Acholi despite the useless fact that the Kenya Luo, is generally closes to the Acholi despite the useless fact that the Kenya Luo, is generally closes to the Acholi. As far as blood is concerned but, perhaps I know what chief Bitek means the word Lango was originally used by the Luo, or refer to the people they encountered on their southward movement but, although the word as derogative denoting.

Savage or people possessed of evil spirits it carried with it a certain amount of respect because, these were the only people who could stand and sometimes even defeat the Luo. In warfare the Kenya Luo for instance recognized only these kinds of people in the world. These are the Luo. Themselves next below them are the Lango such as the Kalenjin the Masii the Teso, etc. them last down the ladder are the Mwa unseless foreigners who could not fight one is either Jaluo-Jalango or Jamwa in that down word order, but, that kind of attitude is not peculiar to be Luo. All tribes had such national pride in them. It is a sentiment however which should no longer have any import but, perhaps I know what Okot means.

The Acholi and the Lango of Ugand are not on the best of terms these days this is now intensified I think by political preponderances but can be said to be a result of childish ideas on the part of the Acholi that a Lango who is not a proper Luo, (smile). Should now rule Ugander and thern claim he is a Luo. Personally I tend and not a blood one, and this would go for Kikuyu-Luhya-Ganda—or Kalenjin. But whether these words coincide in meaning with tribes. I do not know I shall continue to use the word tribe only because, I don't have a better one and only in tell a more discriptistic word been invented our difficulty is aggravated be the fact that the Kenya Luo, for instance are referred to as a tribe and so singly are the Acholi. The Padhola and the Alur and yet all these are but one. They all call themselves Luo., which is the tribe. The smaller unit or the larger one by the same token are the Maragoli-Kisii and Kuria, separate tribe when we know that they are all but Baluhya only georgraphically sundered through historical movements, we could ask the same questions, with regard to the Kikuyu-Embu and Kenda people of the Kenya coast the Baganda-Basoga Baganda-Basoga-Batoro and Banyoro of Uganda Galla Karamojong and Teso and etc.

Our difficulty when he advances the interesting theory that the Luo, of Sudan Uganda, Congo, Ethiopia, Kenya and Tanzania are at a different level. Released to the people formerly called half mamite and who live parallel to them they Karamo jong-Suk-KalenJin-Masia and similar strains in north western parts of Tanzania, I learned all of these people should be referred to simply as Nilotes where that word refers to theirs linguistic kinship if Luo is race. But, if the word tribe is a dangerous one. The theory such as it's only in the best thing which united us in the past where European anthropologists convently fail to see them should echo. For fit suggest that if they should look sharply enough in there east African past they should discover nothing but, that once upon a time they were only one people

This should at preset help them to reject as useless such thing as blood ties it should in the end make it easier for them to develop their former at one minute into a new and more vital cultural unity in east Africa with an indigenous groundwork but, drawing from European oriental friends with whom historical accidents have brought them together and speaking of the Luo tribe they were my good friends while being in Kenya, they supplied me with plenty of my infection we would get in the kitchen that the United States of America government had set aside for me I would be fixing their hair and asking millions of questions about their life, and whatever the question would be. They wouldn't mind sharing them with me.

I am a girl of 14 years of age and the second born child my father died when I was 11 years old and often that no one like men. My mother hates me and won't allow me to go out. I failed in two subjects although last time I failed in five. I tell her this but she just doesn't want me to study. I cook for her keep the rooms clean but, she never like anything I do she keep on scolding me. But I never say a word back to her, she keeps on telling me to die. Please help me for I don't know whether to die or what to do. I told her it is a lot ask a 14 years old girl to try and do, but you have to try to show patience and understanding towards your mother, understand that possible through no fault of your now she might feels resentful toward you, perhaps when your father died she had to worry and work a lot harder on your account and illogically is now venting her accumulated frustration on you so try to be patient with her and allow her time to realize she is being unintelligently and unjustifiable curel to you I the meantime do all you can to help her through what is a crises period in her life by creating as little friction between you as you can. Continue to be helpful in the house and continue to study like any mother she will be instinctively proud of you when you eventually achieve.

I'm a handsome boy 19 years and two years old. I met a girl she loved me and I loved her very much. Our loved lasted about a year until one day she asked me to sleep with her. I refused and I told her I am not interested in the sex game I said to her this should be done after our marriage so she ignored me and after a week I say her with someone else.

Now I'm going steady with another beautiful girl but, even this girl asks me the something to play sex game with her. The problem is that I love her very much and I can't leave her she tells me that if I don't satisfy her she will go with other chaps how can I satisfied her without the sex game. So there is all kinds of hands ups in

Africa. My only answer to his heart warming questions was to now if she feel that way about it is to go ahead and get someone else its worthy sentiment if unusual in this doomed age to want to wait until marriage for sex. What you do about the dilemma depends on the depths of your feeling for her if you really love her and intend marrying her you may have to bow before erective libido or lose her damaging in a bar (smile),

This was a daily occupation answering and asking question. Last Saturday I met a girl who became very friendly to me, she has invited me to a dance which will be held at her house. My problems is I don't know how to dance to this pop music I love this beautiful girl very much and I don't want to lose her at any cost. I told him there was severe courses of actions open. You could stand in a corner watching the dancers with a look of disdain on your face indicating you're about it all or get up a little Dutch carriage and take the girl on the floor all you do then is plant your feet slightly apart shake your hips and move your lips roll your eyes and say it's a beautiful night for dancing. They all ways pay for me. I am very worried about one matter concerning money I have got plenty of friends but, whenever we go to the hotel at picnics they pay the bills although they never ask me to pay. I think it's very bad just to stand by with empty pockets. But you see I'm studying and I don't want to leave school now for low jobs although I get pocket money it's not enough for me and I feel shy to tell my guardians about it. Please tell me what to do. My answer: it is one of those things sunny you're got to grin and bear with the important thing is to continuance of your studies so many youngsters leave school though the lure of money and inevitably they regret it if you r friend begin to get edgy about you non-contribution then you're going to have to start refreshing invitations. But why not have a word in your guardians ear I am sure they won't resent a dioplomatic approach. Have I lost my poet. I am young girl of 15 and lately I made friends with an Ismaili boy whom I love very much: though I couldn't express my love to him. Tuesday this boy asked me to date his mother but, I refused as I was scared of my mother. I did not tell him that but gave him some other excuse lately I have seen this boy with a girl and I am very hurt I was all the more hurt when I thought of the words he said to me. Answer: if our friendship break up, my heart will break the world will break so what will I do to keep our friendship together I know I've had my chance but I was not able to tell him of my feeling what do I do now? Well my Dear, one thing you can make your mind up about straightway, that your dream boat isn't much of a poet why not compose some pose of your own a letter indicating our feeling for him and worries, concerning your mother then set back and wait to see how he receives it.

A shocking situation is worse than a devil. I would like to advise those who are concerned with the implementation of Africanisation especially in the private sector, that should they feel they are unable to do what they are paid for they should resign and give way to more dynamic and practical persons instead of pretending to be doing something, and doing it all wrong giving a wrongful impression that Africanzation is being carried out. I have done a thorough research into Africanization in the private sector and indeed the information. I have gathered is shocking I wonder if my Africans friends would still like me today (smile).

East African, Mombasa Kenya, you have to live by rules and regulations or I should say Americans h ad to live by such rules, here goes when we would go to a movie at a near by theater there is a flag raised, a republican flag of Kenya you must stand at the sign of a bugle in your seat and salute that flag, announced by the Kenya government that is the Kenya law and that is no short cut salute or be detained.

It is no secret that corruption is a worse enemy it is a bigger enemy then the devil is to Christians, unlike contagious diseases however, corruption can be cured if everyone cooperates. I suggest to all men of good will that war be declared against this menace. Like others wars we must be vigilant if we are to win the battle, the struggle will be a long and difficult one. However, we shall neither despair no give in during the fight we should not deceive others like preachers who used to condemn adultery and allies sins every time he delivered a sermon until one day he was summoned to appear in court, charged with getting a school girl pregnant beware of false prophets.

Let's join hands in the spirit of the Lord to get rid of this Devil from amongst our midst remember it is illegal to offer or to receive a bribe the rule applies to all. I respective of individual status in the community the life of a corrupted. Society is very short indeed because, God will not permit corruption to submerge or destroy his will. The corrupted will never escape his punishment when he comes to judge both the living and the dead. Woe unto the culprits.

Finding out what's wrong with Africa, Arabs and Black Muslins and Christians can live in trust the African brotherhood but, the African has to ask themselves what is wrong with our continent in answering this question it is my strong opinion that we should not forget that we have inherited what the colonial power created. It is therefore, very important to bear in mind that most if not all the boundaries of Africa States were created by the colonial power. I strongly oppose the O.A.U. whose constitution stipulates that boundaries in existence after the Independence of Africa, States shall be the legal boundaries while it is very difficult to reorganize new boundaries. Africa should not think it is impossible to undo what the colonial reigns did. What has happen in African since the independence of most states, Sudan to begin with, has experience a tough time to deal with genuine problems.

Par particularly the southern problems the southern blacks feel they cannot live together with the Arabs. Northern they feel the Arabs want to dominate them economically and socially by dominating the government. The Southern African feel the British do no good to combine thing with the Arabs after all the Sudan refugees live comfortably in East Africa. The African people should not forget why the colonial powers did what they have. Inherited and w hat is now the major cause of violent struggle they both assisted African with the motive of divide and rule they knew what weak leaders would cling to, their boundaries after independence and thus keep struggling over what they could easily settle. If the O.A.U. sticks to the present boundaries then I do not see why Dr. Kwame-Nurumahs proposals for accelerating at least Black African were rejected as unrealistic Dr. Nkrumah has clear and practical one government in Africa, is the best solution to African problems of poverty and wars. The U.S.A. is today a top world power but, to unite the U.S.A. cost determined leaders like Lindon Johnson relentless energy and enthusiasm and finally their own lives Africa must unite if it hopes to solve its problems.

Operations: how the girl is operated on, early in the morning the day of the physical operation the girl is called fat cock crow she is fed with a special food called Ckemere-Kia-Como eaten only on this occasion after which she is undressed leaving only one string of beads across her shoulder known as Mogathe-Wa-Mwenji present for the barber. This is given to her sponsor as a symbol of lasting friendship and as a bond of mutual help in all matters it also signifies that hence forth the girl is suppose to hide nothing from her sponsor nor deny her guardian anything demanded from her even if it be the arrangement have been made the girl is escorted to a place appointed for the meeting of all the candidates, from there they are led to a special river where they bathe. The boys assigned to a particular place while the girls bathe at a point below them singing in unison "Togwe-thamba-Na-Munja-Wa-Eeanakc", which means we have bathed with the cream of youth. This is done before sun rises when the water is very cold. They go up to their waist in the river dipping themselves to the breast. Holding up the ceremonial leaves in their hands, then they begin shaking their wrists dropping the leaves into the river as a sign of drowning their childhood behavior and forgetting about it forever. The initiate suspend about half an hour in the river in order to numb their limbs and to prevent pain or less of blood at the time of operation. The sponsors superintend to see that the initiates bathe in the correct manner, while the mothers, relatives and friends, are present painted with red and white.

Ochre-Therega-Iva-Moonyo, singing ritual and encouraging songs. The warriors keep guard to prevent the spectators or strangers from coming too near to the bank. When the bathing completed all the initiates are lined up falling their orders of adoption. The ceremonial horn is blown to warn the passersby that the initiates about to march and that the road must be cleared. No one is allowed to pass across the appointed path as this is regarded as bad luck motion. A small boy and a girl are chosen in accordance with the Gikuyu, believe to be a lucky amen (Nyoni-Ya-Mo-Nyaka) lucky bird, their duty is to carry branches of creepers called Mokenger-Ia and Mwambaigoro, which believed to have certain antiseptic and healing power. The boy and girl with their branches of creepers stand at the entrance of the homestead in order to be the first to meet the initiates on their arrival. As the candidates approach a special ceremonial horn is sounded rhythmically. The initiates advance slowly towards the homestead with both hands raised upwards, elbows bent pressed against their ribs with the first closed, the thumbs inserts between the first and second finger Kuuna-Thano. This signifies that they are ready to stand the operation firmly and fearlessly, unlike the previous day the song take one an entirely different form there is no more dancing and jumping the singing is of a mournful character in slow and gentle voice. This is a moment of great excitement and anxiety, especially for the mother and father.

Whose first born is to be initiated for not only is their boy or girl passing from childhood to adulthood but, the father and mother are to be promoted to be higher status in the society. They all join in singing songs of anxiety. Twahirwoko Tondo-T-Wotongoro, which means where are we led to in this tedious procession in the mean while the elders select a place near the homestead where the operation is to be performed. This place is called Iteeri, here a clean cowhide tanned and polished is spread on the ground. The ceremonial leaves called Mathakwa are spread on the hide the girls sits down on the hide while their female relatives and friends from a sort of circle several rows thick around the girls silently awaiting the great moment no male is allowed to go near or even to peep through this corner and any man caught doing so would be severely punished.

Each of the girls sits down with her legs wide open on the hide her sponsor sits behind her with her inter wound with those of the girl, so as to keep the girls legs in a steady, open position the girls reclines gentle against her sponsor or Motiiri who holds slightly on the shoulders to prevent any bodily movement, the girl mean while staring skywards after this an elderly woman attached to the ceremonial council comes in with very cold water which has been preserved through the night with a steel axe in it. This water is called Mae-Maithanwacaxe water, the water is thrown on the girl sexual organ to make it numb and to arrest profuse, bleeding as well as to shock the girls nerves at the time for she is not suppose to show any fear or make any audible sign of emotion or even to blink to do so would be considered cowardice (Kerogi) and make her the butt of ridicule among her companions for this reason she is expected to keep her eyes fixed upwards until the operation is completed. When this preparation is finished a woman specialist knows as Moruthia, who has studied this form of surgery from childhood dashes out of the crowd dressed in a very peculiar way. With her face painted with white and black orchard. This disguise tends to make her look rather terrifying with her rhythmic movement accompanied be the rattler tide on her legs. She takes out from her packet (Mondo) the operation Gikuyu razor (RwenJi) and in quick movements and with the dexterity of a Harley street surgeon. Proceeds to operate upon the girl with a stroke use cut off the tip of the colitis (Rong-otho) as no other part of the girl's sexual organ is interfered with this complete the girls operation. Immediately the old woman who originally threw the water mixed with some herbs called Mikengeria and

Ndogamoki, which she sprinkles on the fresh wound to reduce the pain and to check bleeding and prevent festering or blood poisoning in a moment each girls is covered with a new dress (Cloak) by her sponsor. At this juncture the silence is broken and the crowd begins to sing joyously in these words. Ciaua-Citto-ire-Kioma-ee-ho-nea-Marerire-ee-ho, which means our children are have ee-hochurra. Did anyone cry. No one cried after this the sponsor hold the girls by the arms and slowly walks to a special called Marerecwa-Mataathi—and Maturanguru. The two first mentioned are used for keeping flies away or any other insect, and also to purify the air and counter act any bad smell which may be caused by the wounds, while the last names is purely a ceremonial herb. The leaves are changed almost daily by the sponsors who are assigned to look after the needs of the initiates (Irui). For the first few days no visitors are allowed to see the girls and the sponsors takes great care to see that no unauthorized person approaches the hut. It is feared that if someone with evil eyes (Grethemengo) sees the girls it will result in illness. Healing of the wound. At the time of the surgical operations the girl hardly feel any pain for the simple reason that her limbs have been numbed, and the operation is over before she is conscious of it. It is only when she awakes after three or four hours of rest that she begins to realize that something has been done to her genital organs. The writer has learned this fact from several girls' relatives and close friends who have gone through the initiation and who belong to the same age group with the rest of them. When the girls wake up the nurse who attendance washes her with some kind of watery herb called Mahoithiac drainers or dyers, after the washing the wound is attended with antiseptic and healing leaves called Kagutwi—or Matei (chasers or banishers the leaves are folded together. About two inches long half an inch wide and quarter of an inch thick then they are dipped in oil) to prevent them sticking on the wound and also to prevent the wound shrinking the bandage is then placed on the wound heals the girls sits down with her legs closed together so as to keep the bandage in position. Frequently the girl is carefully examined by the nurse and whenever she urinates the nurse is there ready to clean the wound and put on a new bandage the old bandage is hidden away to ensure that no man shall cross over it or put his foot on it. For such an act would bring misfortune to the or to the girl. For the first week after he initiation the girl is not allowed to go for a walk or even to touch herself with her bare hands anything in the way of food, the nurse puts the girls food on a banana leaf called Ngoto or Icoya which serve as a plate. The leaf is lifted to the mouth without the girl actually touching its contents with her hands. The food eaten by the invalids is supplied by the parents.

Relatives and friends: the initiates both boys and girls eat collectively all food. Irrespective of where it comes from for all contributions are kept in one place in charge of the nurses and shared in common by the initiates who referred to one another as sisters and brothers. The invalids are entertained by their sponsors who sing them encouraging songs in which they brind out vividly the experience they gained after they were circumcised that in few days their wounds will heal and soon they will be a le to go out jumping and dancing these songs have a great psychological effect on the mind of the initiates for they strongly believe that what, has happen to their predecessors will also happen to them.

With this in view their though rest not on the operation, but on the day when they will again appear in public as full fledged members of the community. On the sixth day the sponsors makes a full report to the ceremonial council, it all initiates are will and can walk a ceremony of Gotonyio or Gociarwo which means to be entered or born is arranged on the eight day. If all are not well the ceremony is postponed until the twelfth day for no ceremony would be arranged or the seventh. Nine of the eleventh day after any event has taken place uneven days are considered by the Giyuyu to be unlucky for embarking or any important business on the day appointed the parents. Gather at the homestead of the (Irua, bringing with Njohi or Ooke) bananas and vegetable the ceremony consists of killing a selected (Ngwaro) which are put on the wrists of the sheep. A ski of which is cut into ribbon (Ngwaro) which are put on the wrists of the boys and girls. The elders who has adopted the children at the time of Irua stands at one side of the entrance of his wife hut, while his wife stands on the other side facing him the rest of the elders and their wives stand in the courtyard in two rows facing one another the children are called to appear before the elders. As they bypass through between the two rows the elders utter blessings and at the same time touch them on the head with sacred leaved called Mataathi and Maturan-Guru at the entrance of the hut the mother and father put the Ngwaro on the wrists of the boys and girls as they enter the hut. After the initiates have entered the hut the mother and father follow them.

The two go to bed while the children remain seated the door (Riigo) is closed and silence is maintained. Both by those inside the hut and those outside in a short moment the mother begins to groan as though she were3 in great pain. The father gets up and open the door quickly he calls out for Mciarithia. A mid wife an elderly woman, who comes in carrying the gut of the sheep which has been killed. It is placed on a hide where the mother is sitting, another woman comes in and cut the gut., at the juncture the boy initiated and the girls join applauding with Ngem I-A-Ri-Ri-Ri-Ri after this the gut is cut into a long ribbon and while the initiated stand in one group close together the ribbon and while the initiated stand in one group close together the ribbon in circle them they stand in this position for a few minutes then the midwife comes along with a razor dipped in sheep blood and the ribbon in two. This symbolizes the cutting the umbilical cord at birth. This is done to express the rebirth o the intitiate another woman then comes carrying ceremonial leave (Mathakwa) sprinkled with blood in which she wraps the ribbon which has just been cut. This is similar to the after birth, and is put on the Mathakwa and carried outside to be buried. When the woman appears outside the parents who are still seated give a round of applause, saying Ciana-Irogea-Ohoro-Thaai-Thathayai-Ngaithaai means peace be with the children, peach beseech Ye-Ngai—(God) peace after this the elder who has adopted the children, they form a big circle round the fire on which the sheep meat has been roasted. An elder of the ceremonial council takes the chest of the sheep which has been roasted (Gethori) and stands up facing Kere-Nyaga, with both hands aloft the elders sings a hymn offering prayers to Ngai, he tears pieces from the meats with teeth, spits them on the ground starting from north, eat south, and west and ending north. He hands over the meat to the elder of the homestead and his wife who follow the same example the two them holding the meat together. Pass it round to each child who tears the meat is the same manner. The elder and his wife address the children as my tribe son or daughter the children answer my tribe father my tribe mother. The Woras used are father to son. "Wanya-Baba" Wakiawa. Son to mother Wakiamaito, mother to daughter Wa-Kia-Mwari, dauther to father Wakia-Baba.

This signifies that the children have now been born again not as the children o an individual, but the whole tribe the initiates address one another as Wanyu-Wakine, which means by tribe brother or sister, when the ceremony is completed all burst into ritual song. They bid farewell to one another and then leave the homestead under the escort of their relatives on the arrival at their respective homes a sheep or goat is killed by the parents to welcome them home again and anoint them as new members of the community (Koinodai-Na-Kohaka-Mwanke or Moiret-Maguta). At this ceremony the parents are provided with brass earrings as a sign or seniority. This is done when the first born is initiated. For a period of three or four mothers according to the rules of various clans the initiates do not participate in any work. They devote most of their time to going around the district singing the initiates, song called Wane in this several groups take part. The songs place in the filled and is performed only in daytime the initiates stand in a big circle holding several sticks (Micee) in their hands. A bunch of Micee is held in the left hand while one stick is held I the right hand. In thy names the initiates beat the Micee-according to the rhythm of the song the inner circle is kept clean for the favorite. From warriors group, mancely those who was the first to reach the sacred tree. They enter the circle two by two a boy and a girl, as they appear in the arena the sticks are beating rhythmically by all, whilst at the same times they utter compliments these meeting offered the initiated boys and girls. Opportunities of coming into contact with the knowing one another intimately. At the end of the holiday period, a day is fixed for the initiates to return to the homestead where the Irua took place here the final ceremony of cleansing or purification is performed. This is called Menjo or Gothiga up to this time initiates have been regarded as children (Ciana) or new comes (Ciumeri), and as such they cannot hold any responsibility in the community for they are in their transitional period. Neither juvenile nor adult laws can be applied to them and thus they from a sort of free community of merry-go-rounds. On the day appointed for the ceremony people gather from far and near to join in the festival dance in which the new comer are introduced into the community the ceremony consists of shaving the head (Kwenda) of the boys and girls. The cloths and ornaments worn during the transitional period are discarded their bodies are painted with red orchard mixed with oil after which they are dressed in new clothes the boys are provided with warrior equipment, the girls are adorned with beads, armlets and others adornments, them they are led to the dance where they are introduced to the assembly are full pledged members of the community. While the dance is going on mother and father partake of a feast of beer drinking (Njohi) which usually takes place during all Salem function.

The wound normally requires a week to heal, but of course there are some cases which takes longer generally due to negligence on the parts of the girls or the noise in applying the healing leaves in the proper way, such as case are few, but result in a septic condition and the formation of much scar tissue on the area of the Labia-Majora which may make child birth difficult cases of this nature sometimes find their way to hospitals and attract the attention of both the missionary and official doctors who then and there without careful investigation of the system of females circumcision attract the custom of clisoridectomy in general asserting that it is barbaric and a menace to the life of the mother, to strengthen their attack on this customs. These well wishers have gone so far as to state the almost every first child dies as a result of this operation at the time of initiation and that the operation it more severe today than it was formerly irresponsible statements of this kind are not taken too seriously for it must not be forgotten that very few of the normal cases of childbirth ever comes to the notice of Europeans doctors.

The theory that every first child dies as a result of the operation has no foundations at all, these are hundreds of first born children among the Gikuyu. Who are still living and the one that I ask so many questions who one of them the missionaries who attack the Irua of girls are more to be pitied then condemned for most of their information is derived from Gikuyu converts who have been taught by these same Christians to regard the custom of female circumcision on something savage and barbaric worthy only of heathen who lives in perpetual sin under the influence of the devil, because of the prejudiced attitude the missionaries are at a disadvantage in knowing the true state of affairs. Even the few scientifically minded ones are themselves so obsessed with prejudice against the custom that their objectivity is blurred in trying to unravel the mystery of the Irua. With such limited knowledge as they are able to acquire from their converts of from others who invariable distort the reality of the Irua in order to please them these some missionaries pose as authorities an African customs how often have we not heard such people saying, we have in Africa for a number of years and we know the African mind well? However, does not qualify them or entitle them to claim authority on sociological or anthropological questions the Africans is in the best position property to discuss and disclose the psychological background of tribal customs such as Irua, etc. and he should be given the opportunity to acquire the scientific training which will enable him to do so. This a point which should be appreciated of the difficulties of field work in narrows parts of the world, sex life among young people.

The physical operation on the genital of both sexes in regarded as a starting point for various activities in the tribal organization on it signifies that the individual operated upon has been given during the course of the perunitation ceremonial dance and songs all the essential information on the laws and customs of the tribe. Among the things taught doing this period all the matters relating to rules and regulations governing sexual indulgence. In order not to suppress entirely the normal sex instinct, the boys and girls are told that in order to keep good health they must acquire the technique of intercourse call Ombani-Na-Ngweko, plantonic love and fondling this form of intimate contact between young people is considered right and proper and the very foundation stone upon which to build a race morally physically and mentally sound for it, safeguards, the youth from nervous and psychic maladjustment. They organize memories night and day dance for recreation and enjoyment at these socials young men and young men mix freely. It is generally at these social gathering that friendship begins, a young man may attract the attention of a young girl or his appearance his smartness in dancing or dressing his hair or by his charming and graceful carriage similarly a young girl may attract the attention of a young man or men, the man who has several girls friends in known a gathering or Keomban (heart breaker). A bear brambly may attack as many as forty girls; a girl may win the admiration of several young men. But they would have to complete for her. The word Ngweko fondling is used in its real Gikuyu sense and not as the loose term Ngweko-Ya-Gecomba employed by missionaries and detribalized. Gikuyu which means full sexual intercourse. In a dance Setharia can easily be recognized for the dance with several girls around him but in order that he will not have a monopoly. A kind of Gikuyu dance Gothombacana, is repeated very often so as to allow the less attractive young man an opportunity of dancing with nice girls. Girls visit their boyfriends frequently especially during the dancing season, the boys also visit the girls in their homes and take them to dances and escort them home afterwards. Ngweko or fondling is looked upon as a sacred act and one which must be done in a systematic well organized manner. The Gikuyu do not kiss girls on the lips as European does, therefore Ngweko takes the place of lip kissing but unlike the Europeans who are found of kissing in public places.

The Gikuyu consider such public display of affection vulgar. All matters relating to sex are done according to well regulated cord of convention, the girls visit their boyfriends at a special hut Thilvgira used as a rendezvous by the young man and woman they bring with them their favorites food and drinks as a taken affection. These are shared among the age group in the Thingira, who eat their food collectively no boy eat or drink by himself what has been brought to him by his sweetheart, such an act would be severely punished in this way the boys would have no girl friends included in all entertainment, because the good looking young man of the age group does not act for himself his popularity is considered the popularity of the group as a whole and his girl friends are also regarded as friends of the members of the age groups so no matter how ugly a boy may be his ugliness is compensated for by the more attractive members of his age group there is a saying in Gikuyui-Mogekumitha-Ka-Kumagiai-Ndotio-Ya-Riira-Ee-Hinya-Riikka-Retire-Gacii when you praise the handsome man. First praise an ugly and strong man of the age group there is no small or despised inferior man in the age group.

Girls may visit the Thigira at any time, day or night after eating while engaged in dramatically to the subject of Ngweko if there are more boys then girls. The girls are asked to select (Kuohanyek) whom they want to have as their companion. The selection is done in the most liberal way for instance the phrase Kuoha-Nyeki to tie the grass which is equalent to choose your partner. In such a case it is not necessary for the girls to select their own intimate friend.

As this would be considered selfish and unsociable of course, this does not mean the girls do not. Sometimes have Ngweko with those whom they are specially from of but generally they follow the rules of exchanging even among married people and for this reason youths are encourage of cultivate the spirit of comradeship and group solidarity before marriage.

After the partners have been arranged one of the boys get up saying Ndathie-Kweno-Gora, I am going to stretch myself. His girl partner follows him to the bed the boy removes all his clothing the girl removes her upper garment Nguo-Ya-Ngoro and retains her skirt Mothuru, and herself leather apron Mweno which she pull back between her legs and tucks in together with her leather skirt Morturu the two V-shaped tails of her Mothuru are pulled forward between her legs from behind and fastened to the waist thus keeping Mweno in position and forming an effective protection of her private parts. In this position the lower lie together facing each other with their legs interwoven to prevent any movement of their legs.

They then begin to fondle each other rubbing their breasts together, while at the same time they engage in love making conversation until they gradually fall asleep, sometimes the partners experience sexual relief, but this is not an essential feature of the Ngweko. The chief concern is this relationship is the enjoyment of the warmth of the breast Orugare-Wa-Nyondo, and not the full experience of sexual intercourse, especially missionaries, that it is unbelievable that a young man and a young woman could sleep in one room let alone in one bed, without copulation.

Many Gikuyu have been punished and regarded as sinners, by missionaries simple for having been found sleeping I the same room with a girl for in their eyes such an act is sinful the Gikuyu who have not been brought up under the missionaries influence find it difficult to understand this sort of European Puritanism for a Gikuyu man have been taught from childhood to develop the technique of self control in the matter of sex, which enables him to sleep in the same bed with a girl without necessary having sexual intercourse. While the missionary's idea is that since a white man would not be able to restrain himself under similar circumstances, so the African would not be able to and so must be forbidden to sleep with a woman friend in Gikuyu fashion.

They then begin to fondle each other rubbing their breasts together, while at the same time they engage in love making conversation until they gradually fall asleep, sometimes the partners experience sexual relief, but this is not an essential feature of the Ngweko. The chief concern is this relationship is the enjoyment of the warmth of the breast Orugare-Wa-Nyondo, and not the full experience of sexual intercourse, especially missionaries, that it is unbelievable that a young man and a young woman could sleep in one room let alone in one bed, without copulation.

Many Gikuyu have been punished and regarded as sinners, by missionaries simple for having been found sleeping in the same room with a girl for in their eyes such an act is sinful the Gikuyu who have not been brought up under the missionaries influence find it difficult to understand this sort of European Puritanism for a Gikuyu man have been taught from childhood to develop the technique of self control in the matter of sex, which enables him to sleep in the same bed with a girl without necessary having sexual intercourse. While the missionaries' idea is that since a white man would not be able to restrain himself under similar circumstances, so the African would be able to and so must be forbidden to sleep with a woman friend in Gikuyu fashion.

The tribal law prohibits a young man from pulling out a girls garment Kugucia-Mwengo-Was-Moiretu while having Ngweko he must put his sexual organ between his thighs so as to prevent touching the girl with it. The custom also prevents a girl from touching the male sexual organ with her hands. Of course it sometimes happens that in the case of a long standing friendship a girl may allow a boy to put his sexual organ between her thighs and hold it tight in that position without penetrating or my mutual arrangement a girl may allow her lover to have full intercourse, trusting that incomplete penetration would safeguard against the tribal law and never take place between casual lovers if it does happen, which is rare the law punishes it by imposing social stigma upon the offenders neither the man nor the girl can sleep with the back turned against the partner the girl may not lie on top of the boy or across him (Gotagarara); to do so or to touch the man's penis is unclean (Mogiro or Thahu). The girl is expected to be a virgin in the since of having an imperforated hymeneal membrane when she marries; any intercourse which may result in pregnancy before marriage is strickly forbidden any young may who may render a girl pregnant (Kiama) tribal council, the fines for this is nine sheep or goats and three big fat sheep (Ndorome) as the Kiama fees besides this the man is made a social outcast or sent to country (Kohingwo) by all the young man and girl of his own age-group punishment is also extended to the girl of her age group she is also liable to ridicule (Kohingwo and Gocambiu). If a man is dedicated by a girly trying to looser her garments during the night a Ngweko she generally reports the matter is taken to the age group meeting (Getongano-Kia-riika). Such a man would be debarred from having Ngweko with other girls as they would not trust or have confidence in him. These guiding principle ingrained in the very souls of the young man and woman serve as checks to sexual promiscuity for unless a man knows a girl very well he would not run the risk of suggesting copulation to her last she could not refuse but, tell others girls and have him (Kohingwoc) sent to country.

Between members of the same family all forms of erratic connection are considered a great sin although there is great freedom among young people in their courtship and amorous experiments. Brothers and sisters would not dare to indulge in these activities in one another presence in bachelor huts where brothers and sisters meets freely but cannot be present together at the sometime, exception purely social occasion when there is no sex play for example if a brother knows that his sister has a lover in a particular bachelor hut he makes a point of not visiting the hut point the same time when she is frequent there, it the same thing applies to the sister the rule is also observed in dance and others ceremonies: no brother could take his sister or any close female relative festival dance, where people from various districts meets and dance together it is not always possible to recognize a relative who come from far away, and a man may sometimes be seen dancing with is cousin by mistake when this happens people who knows will start laughing and joking to warn the young man of his error at once the two separates and find others partners and sometimes a present is given to the girl by way of apology from the man.

All sexual familiarity between parents and their children is strictly forbidden. This applies to all children of the members of one own age. Grade and breath of this rule is considered a great crime, this of course does not restrict parent from teaching their children about sex during early childhood. Parents talk freely to their children explaining all mothers connected with sexual taboos.

In the Gikuyu community any form of sexual intercourse other then the natural from between men and women acting in a normal way is out of the question. It is considered taboos even to have sexual intercourse with a woman. In any position except the regular one face to face. Before initiation it is considered right and proper for boys to practice masturbation as a preparation for their future sexual activities sometimes two or more boys complete in this to see which can show himself more active than the rest. This practice takes place outside the homestead under a tree or bush where the boys are not visible to their elders. It is considered an indecency to be seen doing it except by boys of the same age grade. The practice is given up after the imitation ceremony and anyone seen doing it after that would be looked upon as clinging to a babyish habit and be laughed at because people there is now no need to indulge in it. Among the girls masturbation is considered wrong and if a girl is seen by her mother, even so as touching that part of her body she is at once told that she is doing wrong it may be said that their among her sexual feeling around that point. Holding to these restrictions the practice of homosexuality is unknown among the Goluyu the freedom of intercourse allowed between young people of opposite sex make it necessary and encourage them to acquire experience which will be useful in married life.

Marriage system, in the Gikuyu community marriage and its obligations occupy a position of great importance one of the outstanding features in the Gikuyu system of marriage is the desire of every member of the tribe to build up his own family group, and by this means to extend and prolong his father Mbari (cian). This results in the strengthening of the tribe as a whole. We may mention here that the Gikuyu system of courtship is based on mutual love and gratification of sexual instinct between two individuals and therefore a family is constituted by a permanent union, between one man and one woman or several women though the marriage ceremony a man acquires sole right to sexual intercourse with the woman or women whom he marries on signing the matrimonial contract the marriage ceases to be merely a personal matter for the contract binds not only the bride and bridegroom, but also their kin folks.

It becomes a duty to produce children and sexual intercourse between a man and his wife or wives is looked upon as an act of production and not merely as the gratification of a bodily desire. The Gikuyu tribe custom requires that a married couple should have at least four children, two male and two females. The first male is regarded as perpetuating the existence of the man, father the second as perpetuation that of the woman father. The first and second female children fulfill grandmothers on both sides; the children are given names of the persons whose souls they represent. The desire to have children is deep rooted in the ears of both man and woman and on entering into matrimonial union they regard the procreation of children their first and most sacred duty. A childless marriage in a Gikuyu community is practically a failure for children bring joy not only to their parents but to the Mbari (clan). As a whole in Gikuyu social the rearing of a family brings with it a social status the social position of a married man and woman who have children is of greater importance and dignity then that of a bachelor or spinster after the birth of the first child the married pair become the object of higher regard on the part of their fellows then they were before marriage is one of the most powerful means of maintaining the cohesion of Gikuyu social and of enforcing the conformity to the kinship system and to tribal organization without which social life is impossible the most interesting feeling in the Gikuyu marriage system is the way in which marriage are solemnized for the validity of marriage and the social position of women in the community in determined by the fulfillment of communal duties regulated by the here a full ascriptions of the Gikuyu marriage ceremonies as they are performed today.

There has been some confusion in the minds of many people who have tried to explain the system of marriage and the position of woman in the African community some especially missionaries have gone so far as to say that African woman are regarded as mere chattels of the men well informed anthropologists agree that this is enormous and a misconception of the African social custom. From the following accounts of the institution of marriage among the Gikuyu.

The reader may judge further as to whether purchase is or is not a feature of Gikuyu. Marriage system choice of mates, in the Gikuyu community boys and girls are left free to choose their mates without any interference on the part of the parents of either side from earliest infancy there is chosen social intercourse between the sexes with provides them with an opportunity of becoming acquainted with one another for a considerable judgment in choosing one's husband or wife is almost out of the question.

First stage, when a boy fall in love with a girl he cannot tell her directly that he loves her or display his devotion to her in public as this would be regarded by the Gikuyu. As impolite and uncultured. He therefore discusses the matter with one of two of his best friends in the age group to which he belongs. They then all pay a visit to the girl home on their arrival at the girl's homestead they enter her mother hut. The girl and her mother exchange greetings with them the mother then offers them refreshment and immediately goes away now the boys and the girls are left alone at this stage the conversation may start in the following manner. One of the boys addresses the girl Mware-Wa-Njuguias, daughter of (Nguguna) would you like to ask us why we have come here tonight the girl answer. No it is not necessary to ask you that Gikuyu custom provides that anyone passing by can come and have a meal with us.

The boy that is right Mware-Wa-Njuguna, but we are looking for a homestead where we could be adopted and be given food and shelter not only when we are passing by but, as children of the homestead. at this remark the girl at once knows there object and she asks them to state definitely which one of them is looking for the adoption. The boy then points out his friend who is in love with the girl. If she accepts him as her future husband she tells them to go away and come back some other time. Sometime two or three visits of this kind or made when she gives her final answer she says to them I am willing that the sons of so and so should be adopted into our homestead. But the ceremonial side of it is a matter for my parents you had better talk to them yourselves if she does not accept him she says our house is not big enough to adopt anyone at present and they go away.

If accepted her lover goes home and reports the matter to his parents, they them prepares honey or sugarcane bear which they take to the girls' parents. It is carried in two calabashes one big and the other small. The beer is known as Njohiyanjoorioir, the beer is asking the girl hand, when the parties' meets the first thing the girl parents do is to provide the visitors with food before they go into the question of matrimony. After this they state the object of their visit but, most of the conversation regarding their future son or daughter-in-law is carried on in proverbs. The girl is called and after being introduced she is asked if she have agreed to become engaged, as she cannot answer directly yes or no. a little ceremony is necessary, therefore she is asked gentle to fetch a particular horn used for beer drinking, then he fill it with beer and hand it to her father who after sipping a little and spitting it out, sprinkles some of the beer on his chest, he then hands it over to his wife who does the same. The horn is filled a second time and is handed to the boy parents who repeat the same procedure. In each case the girl takes a sip first as a sign of consent if the lover has been refused the reports to his parents who if they would like their son to marry the girl may visit the girl parents, the same ceremony takes place but if the girl disapproves of it she will not pour out the beer or take the first sip. The visiting parents then go away when the parents initial ceremony is concluded and the girls is willing to be engaged close friends are invited to and the beer is shared among them. At te conclusion of this friendly gathering they are join in a prayer Korathimithia uttering blessings for the future unity and progress of the two families.

Third stage, when the boy parents return home they begin to collect sheep and goats, or cattle if they are rich for the first installment of the dowry Roracio, these would be taken by the lover to the girl's homestead and led to the hut of the girl mother this visit is followed by another in which some beer is brought and the girls is consulted as in the first visit this beer is call Njohiya-Gothugum-theria-Mboriie. The beer for the blessing the Roracio sheep and goats this installments is followed by another in a few days and so on until the number of animals to a out thirty or forty beers is not necessarily brought each time even if a man is rich it is considered ill. Luck to bring all the Roracio at once when according to the custom of the clan, the amount required for sealing the engagement has been sent a day is fixed for the actual engagement ceremony called Ngurarioir. Pouring out the blood of unity, in this all the relatives are called to the girls homestead where a sumptuous feast is provided, which include the slaughtering of a fat sheep (Ngoima-Ya-Ngurario) which has been sent from the boy homestead specially for this purpose. The significance of this ceremony is in the first place to be announced publicly that the girl is engaged. Secondly to provide the relatives on both sides with an opportunity of meeting and getting to decide on how much the Roracio should be. The amount varies from one clan to another and from district to district although the amount required by the Gikuyu law is thirty sheep and goats, sometimes however, it runs to between thirty and eighty sheep and goats apart from numerous presents exchanged on both sides when a cow is included in the Roracio it is valued at ten sheep and goats while an Oz is valued at five sheep and goats. The main feature of this ceremony consists in the killing of a fat sheep kept for this purpose. The main feature of this ceremony consists in the killing of a fat sheep kept for this purpose. The sheep must be on a certain color black, white or brown in keeping with the symbolism adhered to for ritual purposes by the particular clean concerned. The blood is sprinkled along the gateway and towards Mount Kenya (Kere-Nyaga). The contents of the stomach are also sprinkled in the same way, and also on the sheep and goats or cattle which have been brought in for the Roracio. This signifies that they are now purified and protected from any evils and that the boy parents have presented them to the girl parents as a sign of good faith from this time on the interests of the twos clans are closely linked.

Fourth state, after all the arrangements are made in regards to Roracio the maturity of the girl is discussed. The boy parents say to the girl parents, is your daughter grown up yet? Meaning has she menstruated yet? At the end of the discussion a final day is fixed on which to sign the marriage contract on the day in question all representatives of the two clans and friends are invited. They bring with them plenty of food and drinks for the feast the cere3mony which is called Gothenja-Nqoima consists of a slathering six fat sheep and in case of a rich and ox and five sheep.

In doing this the girls consent must be obtained she is asked to provide the knife for skinning the sheep and to take a leading part in slaughtering the first animal. The kidneys of the first sheep are roasted and served to the bride to be who eats them indicating in this way that the engagement still holds good and that the families can proceed with the formality of singing the marriage contract. When this is followed by a big dance and the singing of songs the boy with his age group comes in procession carrying special presents for the girl mother and the members of her clan, any property such as an axe, basket or large leather strap which the girl may have lost as a child will be made up to her parents by these presents at about sunset. After the casual visitors have gone the women representatives of the clan are called into the yards where baskets are kept obtaining their presents. These presents are contributed by one of the elders while the women folks cheer every recipient with great excitement. This is followed by a dance and song called Getiro, for women only, which marks the end of the Ngoima ceremony. If the boy homestead is in the neighborhood a short visit is paid by groups of women taking with them presents for the boy relatives but, if the homestead is far away the visit is left to a later date, from this time onward the girl is regarded as having and been blessing and given away to the boy clan by her parents in agreement with the whole clan. She can now go and weed gardens with the boy mother and others relatives in company with her girlfriend the function of the Ngoima ceremony is to furnish a public wedding celebration in which all marriage agreements are concluded and in which the girl is betrothed to her fiancé, not only by her parents but, the representative body of the clan action collectively she can now be taken to the boys home as his wife. At anytime without any further ceremony being performed at her parents homestead.

Wedding day, when the boy has provided himself with a hut and made the necessary preparation for housekeeping, he approaches his parents especially his mother and ask them to arrange a special day suitable for bringing his wife home the arrangement is made according to certain propitious days at the noon, in accordance with the clans may not hold any wedding between the old and new moon since this period is regarded as a dark period Mweriwenduma the period preferable for embarking on any important project ios the interval between the moon and the full moon.

A Gikuyu wedding is a thing which baffles many outsiders and terrifies many Europeans who may have an opportunity of witnessing the events. This wedding drama misleads foreign on lookers, who do not understand the Gikuyu custom into thinking that the girl are forced to marry and even that they are treated as cattle.

In response to the boy request the family meets in council the day is fixed for the wedding and kept secret from the girl thus adding a dramatic touch to the proceeding on the wedding day the boy female relatives set out to watch the girl movements. She might be in a garden wedding or in forest collecting firewood, etc. When they have obtained the necessary information as to where she is working they search for her on finding her they return with her carrying her shoulder high. This is a moment of real theatrical acting, the girl struggles and refuses to go with them, protesting loudly and even seeming to shed tears. While the woman giggle joyously and cheer her with songs and dances the cries and cheers can be heard for miles around and the Gikuyu people will know that the son of so and so has taken the daughter of so and so in marriage while foreigners may imagine that the girl has been forcible seized if is probably that any person who is not well acquainted with the Gikuyu customs may easily mistake the drama for reality.

In some cases where the families are large, counterfeit fight is stage between the woman of both sides this provides great entertainment for the women and is followed b y a liberal feast at the bridegrooms homestead the girls cries which are uttered theatrically in a singing manner include such phrases as I do not want to get married, I will kill myself if you take me away from my parents, oh how foolish I was to leave my home alone and put myself into the hands of merciless people, where are my relatives, can't they come and release me and prevent my being taken to a man whom I do not love and so on. This goes on until the girl reached the boy homestead where she is led into her new hut while children greet her singing praises for their new bride on her way home the bride is cheered by passersby who utters blessings for the bride and bridegroom and for their feature homestead after the bride is comfortable settle in her new hut the whole parties of women for both clans who a short while ago was engaged in a mock fight join together and start dancing, singing and cheering hilariously, in the evening the bride is visited by her age group of both sexes who bring presents in way of food and ornaments the bride entertains them with songs called Keroie weeping in which girls only takes part while the boys listen. The

Kerero songs are mostly connected with the collective activities of the girl age group and the part played by the girl. It is considered as the age group mourning for the loss of the service and companionship of one of their numbers who by marriage has passed to another age group the mourning songs are continued for eight days during which time the bride is frequently visited by her friends and age group of both sexes. During this period the bride may not go out publicity or do any work. She had a special back path which she may use when she leaves the hut during the day to sit under a tree for fresh air. Her girlfriends keep her company, together with the children of the family the Kerero goes on the whole day and a part of the evening. Except for a few intervals between the arrival and departure of the visitors about bridegroom are left to themselves until the neighborhood of nine o'clock a. m. next morning when the visitors begin to pour in.

The questions of physical virginity as stated in the chapter dealing with the female circumcision in very important and parents excerpt their daughter to go to their husband as physical virgins this must be reported to be parents of both sides. The boy has a show by certain signs that the girl was a virgin the girl too has to do the same to show that the boy is physically fit to be a husband in case of impotency on either side the matter is put before the family's council and the marriage is annulled at once.

On the eighth day when the Kerero ceases a sheep is killed the fat of which is in a ceremony of adoption into the new clan. After she has been admitted as a full member of the husband family she is free to mingle with its members and take an active part in the general work of the homestead when the adoption ceremony is concluded a day is fixed immediately for her to pay a visit to her own parents care is taken in appointing the day, for she must not travel or cook during her menstrual period. On this particular visit she carries a small calabash with bees in it for the use of her parents in blessing her. On her way she is led by a small girl who goes before her holding one end of a stick the other end of which is held by the bride who follows as though she were blind. She is supposed to be unable to see and may not speak to any stranger she may meet doing her journey. She goes all the way with bent head hiding her face shyly. Especially when somebody passes by her she returned back in the evening if the parents are in the neighborhood with presents from her parents. Sometimes three sheep or goats her father-in-law also given her presents, these vary in some cases from five sheep and goats to ten or a cow and a piece of fertile land. These present are regarded as an act of rewarding the bride's but and they end the marriage ceremonial. The Gikuyu customary far of marriage provides that a man may have as many wives as he can support and that the larger ones family the better it is for him and the tribe.

The love of children also encouraging factor of desiring to have more than one wife. The customs also provides that all women must be under the protection of men, and that in order to avoid prostitution no words exists for prostitution in the Gikuyu language all women must be married in their teens fifteen to twenty, thus there is no ferm in the Gikuyu language for unmarried or old maids

Before the advent of the white man institution of seldom and wage workers was unknown to the Gikuyu people the tribal customary law recognized the freedom and independence of every member of the tribe. At the same time all were bound up together socially politically, economically and religiously by a system of collective activities and mutual help; extending from the finally group to the tribe. The welt an shunning of Gikuyu people is Kanya-Gatuue-Ne-Mwamoka-Nero give and take for economic and political reasons every family was expected to be able to protect its own interests and at the same time help the protect the common interests of the tribe from outside attack to do this effectively and to command the respect of the tribe it was necessary for every family to have a number of male children's who could be called up for military services in time of crises and alien aggression. It was also necessary to have a number of female children who could also render assistance by cultivating the land ad looking after the general welfare of the tribe while the men were fighting to defend their homestead furthermore the society cannot do without them for they are the salt of the earth: they have the most sacred duty of creating and reaping future generation female children are therefore, looked up as the connecting link between one generation and another and one clan and another through marriage which binds the interest of clans close together and make them share in common the responsibilities of family life. For this reason say the Gikuyu: Keimba-Kea-Mothni-Na-Mothoni-Igoaga-Hamwe. Liberally corpse of relation in law fall together meaning, together let us live and need be let us die together.

There is a fundamental idea among the Gikuyu that is larger the family is the happier it will be in Kikuyu the qualification for a status to hold a high office in the tribal organization is based on family and not of property as in the case in Europeans society. It is held that if a man can control and manage effectively the affairs of a large family, this is any excellent testimonial his capacity to look after the interest of the tribes whom he will also treat with fatherly love and affection as though his were all parts of his own family thus the saying, Weega-Uum-Aga-Na-Mocie-C. A good leader began his own homestead. After a man has had the first wife, Nyakiami, a year or so generally passes and then his wife start to question him about getting a second wife especially if she is expecting a child or immediately after she has had one my husband don't you think it is wise for you to get me a companion? Moiru, look at your position now. I am sure will realize how God has been good to us to give us a nice healthy baby; Swahili for baby is my little To-T0. I am weak I cannot go to the river to bring water not to the field to grind some food nor to weed our garden, you have no one to cook for you when strangers, you have no one to entertain them. I have my doubt that you realize the seriousness of the matter. What do you think of a daughter of so and so? She is beautiful and industrious and people speak highly about her and family. Do not fail me my husband. Try and win her low. I have spoken to her and found that she is very interested in our homestead. In anything that I can do to help you I am at your service. My husband even if we have hot enough sheep and goats for the dowry our relatives and friends will help you so that you can get her into our family. You are young and healthy and this is the best time for us to have healthy children and so enlarge our family group, and there by perpetuate our family name after you and I have gone. My husband please set quickly as you know the Gikuyu saying mean Mego-Gtherere-MatietaGorere-Mondo-Onyotie, the flowing water of the river does not wait for a thirsty man.

The husband following his wife's advice stats to act. He approaches his parents and after consultation with them arrangements are made to visit the girl parents, if accepted he proceeds to pay the dowry and others gifts connected with marriages when all arrangements are completed he builds a hut next to that of the first wife and then second wife home.

If the family in question is pros porous, after sometime another companion is sought and so the numbers of wives increase from one to fifty and sometimes more. There is no limit of course, this doesn't mean that every Gikuyu man have many wives. There are a large number of Gikuyu men have only one wife simple because, there economic position would not allow them to have as many wives as they society would like. Taking the Gikuyu population as a whole it can be said that there is a average of two wives per head, owning to the numbers of women who attain the marriageable age. Women generally marry between the age of fifteen and twenty. While the majority of men started marrying from the age of twenty-five thus in every generation there age more women of marriageable, age then men, which helps to balance the system of polygamy.

The management of a household has his own hut (thingira) in which friends and casual visitors are entertained each wife have her own hut where she keep her personal belongings the cooking is also done in it while collective ownership in a fundamental principle of the family group. The hut is considered as the private property of the wife and it is entirely under her control. Each wife is provided with several lots of land located in different places within the boundary of the family land allotment the woman usually cultivate banana, sugarcane, sweet potatoes, maize, millet yams, several varieties of beans and other crops on these holdings the working of the land is collective men doing the clearing of the virgin soil. Such as cutting big trees and hoeing while women come behind them tearing the soil to prepare if for planting. The plating is also divided between men and women the men take the responsibility of planting banana, sugarcane yams, and sometimes sweet potatoes the women plant millet, maize various kinds of beans and potatoes. The last are planted by both sexes. Each wife is responsible for what she produces from the land and can distributed is as she pleases provided that she has reserved enough food for the use of herself and family until the next harvest.

She can sell any surplus stock in the market and by what she likes, or keep the proceeds for family purposes nowadays the majority of their hut taxes in this way. Sometimes, when the harvest is good and there is an abundant supply of products some are handle over to the husband who buys sheep, goats or a cow for the betterment of the homestead.

While the division of personal property exists between the wives the husband is the head of the family and the one who contributes his labor power to all equally. He belongs to all and all belong to him. This brings the division to one collective ownership under his guidance having described the division and distribution of labor it is necessary to mention something about the distribution of love. No doubt some people wonder how one man is able to love many women. This is a very vital question especially among those whose religious beliefs have taught them that to loves are more than one woman is a crime and the Gikuyu are taught from childhood, that is to be a man is to be able to love and keep a homestead with as many wives as possible. With this in view Gikuyu male children are brought up to cultivable the idea and technique of extending their love several women and to look upon them as companions and as members of one big family the girls are too taught how to share a husband's love and to look upon as the father of one big family. The idea of sharing everything is strongly emphasized in the upbringing of children so when they grow up and affection with others for it is said that to live with others is to share and to have mercy for one another, and it is witchdoctors who lives and eat along. In order to avoid jealousy (Oiru) among the wives. Gikuyu custom provides that each wife must be visited by her husband or certain days of the moon, particularly the three following menstruation each wife has this special privilege. The wives knowing that this is the best time to have children see to it that the husband does not neglect his duty of distributing his love equally among them such conjugal relation is the only way in which a polygamous homestead could be kept in harmony.

The three days immediately after menstruating are considered as the most likely for a woman to conceive for this reason the husband does not general cohabit with her again until after the next menstruation if by then she has conceived the husband allows a period of three months, to elapse before having intercourse again in order not to cause an abortion after this time the husband may cohabit with her but only in a special way that is he must not have full penetration he may use only about two inches of his penis the limit is indicated by a process in the Irua operation when the operator gather back the foreskin into a tassel called Ngwati the bush which is arranged to hang at the right distance below the head of the penis its use is to increase sexual excitement but it can also serve as a catch to check penetration fuller penetration is believed to result in destroying the womb.

Duty of the wives, the women are essentially the homemaker as without them there is no home in the Gikuyu since of social life each wife has a special duty assigned to her in the general affairs of the homestead. She is responsible for looking after her hut and her household utensils, granary and her garden. But the duty of looking after the husband is such as cleaning his hut supplying him with firewood, water, food, etc. is shared by all in turn. For example every morning one of them cleans the husband hut (thingira) and lights the fire. While others sweep the yard and do other work connected with the cleanliness of the homestead at the same time, sheep and goats are few, cow if they have any are milked calves and kids are tented.

The husband is served with food according to what they have prepared. Each wife provides food for her children, when the morning work in the homestead is over. Each wife is supposed to prepare a plan of activities for the day, some go to the forest to collect firewood other go to cultivate their gardens, relatives or individually. During the day time everyone is engaged in some sort of activity or another no one stays at home except the small children who are unable to accompany the adult member of the family to the field, of those grown up who engaged in some home worker. Especially that a grinding of beating grain in mortars. In the evening the wives return home carrying various things firewood water, banana, sweet potatoes, yams and other food stuff. Immediately they set about preparing food for the evening meal. The wife whose turn it is provides the firewood and lights the fire in her husband hut, no cooking is done in that hut except, when meat is roasted otherwise each wife cooking is done in their own hut. When the food is ready each wife takes the husband share to his hut where he entertains his friends and casual visitors when the meal if over and utensils cleaned the wives may go and spend the rest of the evening in the company of their husbands or remain in their huts. But whenever special visitors particularly members of the husbands age group call the wives are expected to join the company in the husbands hut. The reason for this is to show the solidarity of the age group if the visitors come from far away, and they are to spend the night in the homestead. The arrangement for their accommodation are made according to the rules and customs governing and social affairs among the age group. On these occasions the wives exercise their freedom, which amounts to some things like polyandry. Each wife is free to choose anyone in the age group and give him accommodation for the night.

This is looked upon as purely social intercourse and no feeling or jealousy or evil is attached to it on the part of the husband or wife and having all been brought up and educated in the idea of sharing especially at the time when they indulged in Ngweko love making their hearts are saturated with ideas of collective enjoyment without which there could not be strong unity among the members of the age groups when this choice is freely exercised, it is an offense for a wife to invite man secretly to her hut even a member of the age group, to so would be regarded oneself as committing adultery in order to guard oneself against matrimonial injuries this custom is strictly adhered to any man who is caught breaking the rule is punished heavily by the Kiama and sometimes the husband takes the law into his own hands and before the Kiama punishes the offender he is given a good beating by the outraged husband. There is a saying in Gikuyu which says that before a man embarked upon such an adventure of visiting another man's wife it is advisable for him to arm himself for there is no mercy for one who entices another man's wife or steal his cow (Ngombelvaakaitire-Ndogo) the wife too punished she is taken back to her parents who in order to establish good relationship have to pay a fine of one or two goats to the husband the fine is followed by a feast or beer drinking between the two family sometimes if this offense is repeated the wife is divorced and the husband is entitled to get back all his Roracoio, with the interested and custody of his offering the divorce is preferred especially in a case where there are no children but, in the case of partners who have children. Conciliation is considered and the best procedure for in this case the matter has already ceased to be between individuals and has moved into the clan. Thought the children for children are regarded as the pledges of love and unity. It is only when the matter becomes really bad that divorce action is taken. We will deal with the divorce question later under Megior attached to the cohabitation of a married woman and the social stigma which follows an offense the breaking of this law is very rare.

This is due to the fact that both wife and husband have ample opportunity of meeting their friends in a more open and legalized way, approved by the moral code of the community. It is worth our while to mention a few of these taboos Megiro which control the relationship between a married woman and an outsider and even the husband for example it is Mergiro for a wife to have sexual intercourse outside the homestead this is considered as bringing evil and bad luck to the homestead no wife may have sexual intercourse while her husband is way on a journey, or war or other activities, for to do so is to cause misfortune to the husband. No sexual intercourse while food is being cooked for this will make the food impure and the result to those who would eat such food would be uncleanliness. Children must be put to bed before this sexual intercourse is not held to be right if the children are away in the field, for it is considered as a ritual shutting out the children (Kohingereriaciana). Sexual intercourse is practiced ritually and these and many others Megiro are considered important and in order to maintain the harmony and prosperity of a husband and to guard themselves against matrimonial injuries in the community those Megior (taboos) must be rigidly observed among the Gikuyu divorce is very rare.

Because of the fact that a wife is regarded as the foundation rock on which the homestead is built without her the homestead is broken therefore, it is only when all efforts to keep the homestead and wife together have failed that an action for divorce can be taken. According to the Gikuyu customary law a husband may divorce his wife on the grounds of (1) bareness (2) refusal to render conjugal rights without reason (3) practicing witchcraft (4) being an habitual thief (5) willful desertion (6) continual gross misconduct. A wife has the same rights to divorce her husband on these same rights ground except (7) owning perhaps to the system of Polygram, besides the above mentioned ground she can divorce her husband for cruelty, ill treatment, drunkenness and impotence. In the case of bareness or impotence both husband and wife go through practical test to prove who is to blame. The husband would allow his wife to have sexual intercourse with one or more of his age group if this fails to bring fruitful result a medicine man of repute (Mondo-Mogo) is consulted with the hope of finding a successful solution. At the same time ceremonial blessing from parents on both sides is considered essential to fertilize the womb. Sometimes the wife succeeds in having a child in this way and is saved from the embarrassing situation of being given a nickname of Thaafa (Barren) but when all efforts fail the case is considered as one above the power of men and is attributed to the will of Ngai, the great god, if there is no other disagreement between the husband and wife the two can live together and perhaps have an adopted son or daughter providing that the man is not in a position to marry another wife.

In case of impotency the man is given the same trial as the woman if he can afford if it is necessary to marry another wife and in case he succeeds in having children by his first wife is due to the fact that their blood does not agree. But if a man knows that he is naturally impotent and wishes to keep his homestead in harmony h allows his wife or wives to have sexual companions of friends to fulfill the duty of procreation the children of such a union are regarded exactly in the same way as if the real husband had been physically fit to function sexually.

When a wife is ill treated by her husband she has the treatment is proved, the father for protection if the ill treatment is proved the father may keep his daughter in his homestead until such time as the homestead pays a find and promises not to ill treat his wife again. If a wife has borne a child the husband cannot clan his property which he had given as Roracio, but in case of divorce the child is always left with the father. If the woman marries again her former husband has the right to claim at least half of his sheep and goats of cattle. But if she remains in her father homestead and perhaps has friend no property can be claimed on the other hands if she happens to have a child during that time the former husband claim that child as his for as long as Roracio is not returned the union is not completely dissolved. When there are no children in a matrimonial union the separation or divorce in such a simpler than otherwise in the Gikuyu system of marriage the presence of children is a sure sign of keeping the two coupled together in harmony.

Four die in tribal battle, tribesman from Poket and market clashed at Chesegon Market in Kapenguria and as a result four people was killed and eight wounded. A police reported and stated yesterday; the Poket are believed to have stolen 93 cows and 256 goats. It is understood that tension between both tribes in the area is running high police are patrolling the area. Another police report said that Mr. Tsivo of Eldoret told the police that his night watchman was attacked by a gang of robbers who tied him up brooked into a shop and stole property valued at $600 shillings police later arrested two men and property valued at $600 shillings were reported.

It's all horse and no carriage for African women. This situation today is that women are always blamed for unhappy marital relationship. Women are always nagging women are domineering and their place in the family; women are unfaithful, women are too demanding, women makes marriage life extremely difficult. This is the popular belief and for specific here are some historical example:

Euenie Napoleon destroyed a promising marriage by her countess Toistoi nagged her husband to death. Mrs. Abraham Lincoln ruined a would have been happy marriage by her nagging. But while all these allegation may be true, and nobody is denying that they are. Women given a fair deal does anybody ever bother to prove into the situation in an effort to find out the whole truth of the matter. Does anybody ever try to find out whether sometimes men might be just as guilty as women if not more? I don't know enough about other countries but, in Kenya the issue is quite clear cut women are always responsible for unsuccessful marriages. Modern African husbands are always right, they are faultless demigods and they the right to humiliate, mistreat and even beat their wives, and as a wife, you are supposed to take these indignities and injustices with a smile. You are expected to forget experiences immediately you are through with them and carry on with normal life as if nothing has happen. Everyone will definitely agree that African husbands are not lacking in Christian charity turn the other cheek forgive and forget. A wife can never feel hurt or offended. A wife should realize that her husband has an inalienable right to frustrated her, to show her how stupid she is to make her feel extremely small unimportant and unwanted. The husband has a right to offend to hurt, to torment, to crucify, after all the wife wears his ring to remind herself that she is his own property. One of his many possessions and he can do anything he likes with her, and no matter how right the wife might be she should never answer back of criticize.

Instead she should take everything happily without arguing because, after all she vowed to love, honor, and obey. Therefore, when the husband comes home dead drunk at three o'clock in the morning from business negotiations the wife is supposed to embrace him warmly and ask him how was work today darling? The trouble is that she doesn't know which is correct yesterday or this morning, but she may anything so long she doesn't criticize her husband. When on his way out to the bar the husband authoritatively tells his wife he has no money for groceries she is supposed to send him off happily with a have a nice time honey. When he brings his glamorous mistress the wife is expected to entertain her and when the husband tells his wife to catch a bus home, because he has got to meet some of the boys she is suppose to do just like that unless she can afford a broken jaw in the evening. A woman can go shopping by bus, a woman can take children to hospital by bus, a woman can go to work by bus, ironically to earn money which is not really hers to spend as she like.

Why simply because, a car whose maintenance is a family affair is beyond her aspirations. Therefore the wife should feel proud that she is married to a man who owns a car for his and his friends comfort and convenience she should consider traveling by bus a great honor because, she comes from a poor family. Indeed this woman ought to appreciate the fact that she has been rescued from the gutters.

Many African men expect their wives to be knowledgeable, humorous fashionable and up to their standards. Still these same husbands don't appreciated what their wives achieved as a matter of fact, not only do they resent their wives aspirations but they also suppress the trouble with many African husbands therefore, is that they want to have their cake and eat it too. Get married to educated women but they resent their sensitive somewhat sophisticated ambitious personalities. Very unfairly they demand that there should live their father and grandfather. These men tend to forget that all these sacrifices which their wives made to acquire education were a means to an end. They were a passport to a more gratifying and comfortable life. Paradoxically after denying all this husbands expect their wives to contribute to family income of course by utilizing the very. Education which is being undermined and once the money is earned the wives are expected to forget all about it. Now what can we make out these self contradiction. I don't really don't know but, observing that many African husbands are misfits they are so confused that they don't know who they are or whither they are gone.

Some of them do things not as an application of their own philosophy but, because their colleagues are doing them. Surprisingly they imitate the condemnable and completely ignore the commendable many African husbands are so ambiguous that while on the one hand they pose like educated, smart-looking respectable gentlemen on the other they behave like uncultured men. In the final analysis therefore, it seems as it social progress has turned them into heartless. Egoistic unappreciative creatures who are too proud to admit their weaknesses and mistakes or make an apology.

Under the pretext of safeguarding themselves against the popularly condemned domineering wives, they will devise legitimate ways and means of releasing their professional frustrations on the willing horses their better halves. Unfortunately the greater truth is not that they are used by feminine domination but that they greatly fear that if they habitually take their wives into their confidence this will one day betray their objectionable indulgences. Eventually these wives are driven into the background from where they watch the nerve wracking drama, unfortunately, these women not only worry about their children future but, they also see new marriages in the unfavorable light of their own and feel sorry for the young captives. At any rate these wives endure their miserable lives for the sake of their children no woman suffer. Many others preserve because, they have hope that one day things will change for the better.

They are hopeful that the life they have chosen which now seems a necessary evil will one day be something to be their womanhood, but of their past hope is their life blood because, they realize that even if they run away from the ordeal, they will never be their pre-marriage selves again.

Absorbing look at African marriages: ever since Adam walked up to Eve in the Garden of Eden and announced Madam I'm Adam the world has never been the same. Many of the ideas a reader has clung to before reading the authenticate and well documented book will definitely change probably for the better after reading it.

It is an excellently written piece of sociological literature which gives a comprehensive background to married life in West Africa, particularly Ghama which in many cases in identical with many others Black African Countries.

The author Dr. T. Peter Omorie of Ghance University is an authority of international repute in the field of sociology of extensive disciplined, devoted and continuous research. Few of the correspondents to such popular columns known as advice to the

Loverlorns realize that their letters provided quite useful material for students of sociology when doing their research in problems pertaining to romances marital difficulties neuroses adolescence and domestic chores. Omori has set out his argumental in a highly logical manner which makes admirable reading. Its English is attractive and the book is well expounded. It even includes a reference to President Kenyatta's book-facing Mount Kenya youngsters practice self-abuse openly. It also interesting to compare traditional, Africa married life with modern married life as influenced by the western civilization and Omori successfully, provides such discussion. Problems of adolescence love definitions of dating and courtship the legality of marriage and the effects of divorce are intelligently and logically discussed with profound knowledge. It is a book which deserves a highly respected place on the shelf of sociological literature and Omori's contribution to this field is highly commended.

The whodunit I supposed is the category into which the Afersata and Ethiopian novel to be placed. Except that traditional whodunits usually end with the disclosure of the villain after leading us up many false traits. In this book we are shown a suspect but, we never really find out whodunit who set fire to Namaga's hut and stole his money.

The Afersata the traditional way of investigating crime is an utter failure and a time consuming nuisance to the whole community. In fact the plot is little more than vehicle for Sahle Seiassis delicate cames of Ethiopian village life. The author brings out the semi-feudal rigidity of the social and political systems as it affects humble villagers. The nepotism of Ethiopian ancient system is also well conveyed with the good for nothing suspect Beshir leaning heavily on the reputation of his Uncle Melesse who actually works in Addis Ababa. Selassie who never avoids relevant social comments, also has critical remarks to make of the land tenure system. This book however is note political tract by any means it gives the readers an insight that rings true into a unique and historic country of Africa.

Mombasa summit, tomorrow President Kenyatta of Kenya will play host in Mombasa to the other two members of the East Africa authority. President Oboto of Ugander, and president Nyereae of Tasnzan, also present will be President Kaunda whose country Zambia has now every chance of becoming the fourth member of the East African community. The gathering in Mombasa of the big four is primarily to witness the commissioning of M. V. Mulungushi, solemn rite at which President Kaunda himself will officiate. But more than that the frequency with which the leaders of the East and Central African countries meets of consultations with each other is a constant indication of their desire for continued co-operation and good will within the framework of the East African community.

From time to time there has been idle talk that the community is in danger of falling asunder. Mention has been made for example of Kenya being unfair to her partners in matters of trade of that Kenya was too far ahead of the other two in economic cooperation. It has also been observed that Tanzania and to a less extent, Uganda and Tanzania could have claimed that Kenya was trying to go it alone in the recent locomotive purchase controversy.

Let this be as it may. The important thing to note is that the community like any other large organization is bound to have its inner anomalies. Some of which the contractual parties could not have helped at the beginning because, they were caused by historical difference. But to the point out these anomalies, as each of the members countries have often done. Must not be confused with the wish to break away, to express divergent opinions within the broad outlines of an organization is a sign of health it is the good sign that they are a mature society talking to itself. The accusations of dissidence leveled, for example, at Uganda for the proposed break-up of the University I cannot subscribe to. They do not believe that if constitutes a real break-up it is the logical development of an institution which has out grown its terms of reference for there is no doubt that East Africa has begun to need even many more separate Universities then three. What they must realize is that because of the desirability of the whole none of its single units can afford to go too astray.

Tansinia and Zambia has been accused of moving to far away to the left. Kenya it has been said has remained too rightist but each sovereign states has a right to choose its own system so long as this is not to inconsistent with postulates of the whole. We believe that the importance of the community will finally prevent any further drifting apart. This may become true and true if the other applicants such as the Congo Burundi, Ethiopia, the Sudan and Somalia, are finally allowed into their fold. For each will bring with it peculiar benefits which might draw them closer then they may realize now, such as the Congo's and Zambia so minerals Sudan's cottons Somalia's livestock and bananas East Africa tourism. Ethiopia's coffee etc.

While it is true that the community has a number of inherent inconsistencies of organization and is composed of countries in different stages of development it would still be in their communal entrust. While pointing these out and trying to correct them to save this international organization whose very existence is witness that it is of benefit of all of them.

Ban all tourist visits to Masailand the question of Masailand as a tourist, attraction is a very intriguist one. Last week it was raised in parliament but what surprised me most was that those who are supposed to know better like Mr. Oloitipitip did not look at the issue objectively. Many people are not opposed to Masai owning cattle or even gaining some money from tourists in a way that does not embarrass those genuine Kenyans who want this nation considered as a nation of human elements. What is the attitude of those who come to watch leopards, lions, and giraffe and then move to Masailand to go and watch the Masai? Do you earnestly believe their attitude towards the Masai is any difference from that of Rhinos?

Well people like Mr. Olitipitip will say does that matter. Yet they will be the first to object if the Masai were to be considered as anything else, and do they realize how these tourists snap their cameras at the sight of a Masai not so much as his beauty and naturality bust as a specimen of the primitive peoples inhabiting the Dark Continent. I say do Masai leaders and all others realize the psychological factors that arise from watching the Masai? We should uphold the dignity of our nation. The government should first and foremost ban photography in Masailan and if possible ban all tourist visits. Surely we are not going to lose half our revenue because, the Masai visits are banned and if we are to follow Mr. Oloitipitip's story, the Masai will not lose much since they are rich cattle owners and a loss of a few shillings will not make a difference. The whole issue revolves over human dignity. I would not have opposed Masailand as a tourist attraction had the attitude of the tourists not been conditioned by the colonial past to look upon the African as a sub human being, and if the situation is being perpetuated because of a few extra shillings are we earnestly upholding the dignity of our nation? Does an American tourist from the deep south who does not even consider a Negro his equal watch the Masai as a human being or vice versa. These two answer frequently.

Nation building a widely used words but least understood has many facets it is not only economic progress that constitutes nation-building. The molding of all the different people and communities within the domain of this country into one people is in itself nation-building. Continual maintenance of National pride and dignity would be an over aspect of nation building, and integral part of it. The development of the nation both physical and psychological must be maintained throughout the entire country Masailand must not be excluded. It is apparent that there government is definitely, but unconsciously, sciously, secluding the Masai area as a tourist attraction only.

Guiyu tribe, in case I didn't mention this about the Guiyu tribe women they wear a bridle over their head made on the order of a mule bridle it is made of leather like an American mule this is to help carry and balance their belonging and their heard tell me how many times we didn't see this with their husbands walking right beside his wife carrying noghint but a walking cane. While his wife carries a jackass load. Belonging on head five gallons of water in each hand in canes that they call Jerry canes and a baby strapped to their backs in their language toe-toe means baby.

Court sees live goat in Masai murder trial, a blood stained "rungu", a spear, a goat and goat's skin were among several exhibits produced before the high court sitting in Nairobi yesterday during the trial of three Masai tribesmen charged with murder. The accused Kemari: Ole Pulei Parmunkyo Ole Kararku and sunkau Ole Musei are charged that one Number 2nd last year they jointly murdered Meitigin Ole Chenoigu at Matathia reserve, Kajiado. Police CPL. Tirias Mweresa told Mr. Kneller that on November 12th he and six others police officers attacked to Ngong police station were instructed to go for investigation in connection with stock theft.

They went to a Masai Man-Yatta and on entering one of the huts, found the first accused sitting there with his mother in the hut, he said was a white billy goat which was identified by the wife of the deceased as belonging to her husband.

Getting the Masai to change your editorial, a amtterof dress (August 9th, 1969) cannot go unscrutinised. The whole theme seems to be opposed to "cover yourself up government". In other words you suggested that we should keep the Masai "naked" rather in the posture they have been so as to attract and boost the tourist industry. I would term this suggestion apathetical of course it is true that tourism is the major source of revenue not only in Tanzania but also in all East Africa. However it should be remembered that we are all human beings with equal status in the eyes of God and I don't remember anywhere in the bible where it is written that the Masai would be used as an attraction to Europeans. Therefore, we are not going to allow the boosting of the economy at the expense of the Masai people. It is an undeniable fact that the Masia still retain their tradition as far as clothing is concerned. This is as a result of their being late in getting into modern life so as to fit into society.

Making the Masai change civilization still this does not rule out the fact that they should be encouraged and uplifted by the rest of the community to modern life so as to fit into society. I totally disapprove of the way this has been done. I suggest that this should have been done not by force but by way of persuasion and by explaining to the Masai why they should wear clothes. A Masai in his lion cloth does not fit into our society, although we cannot expect them to be happy in suits and so forth. Due to the heat and nomadic way of living we must accept the fact that dressing is an adopted culture. Therefore this should not be an excuse for leaving the Masia as they were half a century ago. Even we, who are civilized, tend to misuse our civilization. Take for example Nairobi, there are people who wear a suit shirt and tie all year round, I assure you that these people do not enjoy it but just because they see a British in England and an American in the same style they imitate him. They do not take into account the climatic conditions of a particular country or place, are you aware if you are an African, as you say that long ago our forefathers wore animals skins diagonally on their bodies, and that these day their sons you and I are differently dressed. What do you think has led to this? Why can't the same apply to the Masai people. I mean to say that your article, "A Matter of Dress would better have been" a matter of civilization while accepting foreign ideologies we should not forget our own culture. At the same time we should examine and see why certain people do certain things and where. This will help us to be good judges to choose only what is good for our society.

God was kind enough to give East Africa, with its magnificent features and game and safeguard the same for tourists but not to turn themselves into moving museum for them.

From the president himself he tells it like it is what trouble will not be tolerated in Kenya. Mzee Jumo Kenyatta in Kenya in his speech at an opening of the Kisumu hospital. President Kenyatta began by praising the Russians for donating the new hospital which he said had not been opened before although it had been operating for a while because, of this or that problem. We come here to bless Nyanze because of what Kanu have done not because of anything that KPU hoped to do. He said K.P.U. is only engaged in dirty divisive words I know that Odinga is my friend and he fought for my release and he in turn continues to mislead the people of this area.

Kanu rules and I would have detained him a long time ago. To show him that we have power, but I cannot do so because, I respect our personal friendship. But I can assure you my brothers that anybody who brings trouble in Kisumu or anywhere in Kenya will be taught to know that Kenya have a government.

President Kenyatta at this point faced Mr. Odinga personally and said Oginga you do not tell us where Dume is going, but Kanu tells the country that this is an Independent Kenya. Since you K.P.U. do not tell us where you are going we are going to crush you into floor. President Kenyatta said that by opining this hospital he had come to show the people of Nyanza progress anybody who plays with our progress such as K.P.U. tries to do will be crushed like locusts, he said.

The president faced Mr. Odinga again and sad Jaramogi do not say later that I did not warn you publicly and I warn you once more that if I did not know you personally, I would have shown you that I do not indulge in child play, so you must stop this child play. He went on in Kenya we want only safety unity and prosperity for the Wananchi and the government will rule forever because, of these principles, because what Wananchi knows that K.P.U. people are like floating clouds they do not know where they are going. At this point the crowd roared in a confused noise to which the president replied angrily. Stop there or I'll come down and crush you, you were making a noise for nothing and you should know that Odinga is just as much a noise maker who is good for nothing.

The president told the audience that he had visited Kisumu because; he had a basic love for Kisumu people as much as for all Kenyans and the whole world. He blame the present trends of disunity on the Europeans the Wazungu who had come to Africa with the policy that this man was different from that other man so that he could rule. The Europeans wanted the doctrine of divide and rule so that he could rule more effectively. At this point he again faced Mr. Odinga and said, you are rich while the people of Nyanza re starving. Mr. Odinga replied: but we are hungry, despite the government's promises Mr. Kenyatta said: you are hungry because, you do not want to, you have got people to expect free things. I Kanyatta am self sufficient at home. The president then said that Mr. Odinga was his student in politics but, he did not know what had gone wrong with his head. A section of the people shouted; let him go back to Kanu. President Kenyatta then chuckled you know I did not expel him form Kanu he went away of his own accord. I am not going to ask him to come back to Kanu. He knows it is his duty to do so. Referring to the disturbances that has earlier taken place between security police and the unruly crowd President Kenyatta said: today some of you have tasted our strength we are going to treat all troublemakers likewise. President Kenyatta ended by saying that by donating the hospital the Russian people had proved that they were good people. They have big hearts and only want to help Africans although there are African who want to use the Russians for their own games he said. How well do I remember it was a frightening time for us who was there in Kenya at the time this was in October 27, 1969.

Blind African man killed wrong person was sentences to be hung: a blind man who vowed revenge against his brother killer but slew the wrong man is to hand the high court has decided at Dodoma Central Tanzania. The court was told that after a party the brother of Lemutya-Hoteya, the accessed was killed by an arrow. Hoteya heard of this and set out to find the killer when he arrived at the house where the party had been held he assumed it was the owner. Jobe Buu who had killed his brother. He speared Buu, thru the shoulder, but it was not Buu who had committed the crime. Hoteya is to appeal to the East African court of appeal against his conviction for murder.

I am hoping whosoever read my book will get a great deal of interest facts out of it. God Bless and Keep you. Thank you Jambo-Hello—Quahali-Good-bye.

What inspired Mrs. Armstead to write well its make me no different about the critics I have broad shoulder Hi Hi.

There is plenty to write about, talk about and learn about.

I am writing from my own eye experience because I had servants two weeks after my husband and I arrived on this island.

Being so excited about going to East Africa. I had read about it in school.

There are definition and word of the Swahili Language.